THE LEGAL STUFF

Copyright © 2024 by Ben Levy

All rights reserved.

No portion of this book may be reproduced in any form without written permission from the publisher or author, except as permitted by U.S. copyright law.

This publication is designed to provide accurate and authoritative information in regard to the subject matter covered. While the publisher and author have used their best efforts in preparing this book, they make no representations or warranties with respect to the accuracy or completeness of the contents of this book and specifically disclaim any implied warranties of merchantability or fitness for a particular purpose.

No warranty may be created or extended by sales representatives or written sales materials. The advice and strategies contained herein may not be suitable for your situation.

Neither the publisher nor the author shall be liable for any loss of profit or any other commercial damages, including but not limited to special, incidental, consequential, personal, or other damages.

Snooooooore. C'mon, let's get to the good stuff.

Book Cover by Kelly Bartell

Design by Andrew Mark Lawrence

STOP READING SLIDES

HOW TO NAIL CREATIVE PRESENTATIONS AND SELL YOUR BEST IDEAS

By BEN LEVY
With foreword by Greg Hahn

DEDICATION

To my mother, for showing me how to build a story,

And to my father, for showing me how to tell one.

TABLE OF CONTENTS

(Utterly useless in presentations. Significantly more useful in books about presentations.)

4 Foreword

7 **Introduction** I am not a natural presenter

8 **Stop believing ideas sell themselves (Part 1)**
10 Start Recognizing Why Clients Buy Bad Ideas
14 **Stop using templates (Part 2)**
16 Start Thinking Of Presentations As Ads
22 Start Using The Story That Always Wins
38 Start Leveraging The Invisible Brief
48 Start Planning For Half-Time
56 **Stop calling your concepts equal (Part 3)**
58 Start Sharing Multiple Ideas Intentionally
61 Start Taking Straw Dogs Behind the Barn
61 Start Choosing Favorite Children
64 **Stop trying to memorize (Part 4)**
66 Start Thinking In Bullets
71 Start Using Slides As Notes
72 Start Trusting Yourself
74 **Stop explaining ideas (Part 5)**
76 Start Putting Wow Before How
81 Start Being Generally Right Over Perfectly Correct
73 Start Using Analogies And Metaphors
86 **Stop fabricating drama (Part 6)**
88 Start Using Suspense Over Surprise
91 Start Avoiding Words Like Epic, Awesome, And Amazing
92 **Stop using infographics (Part 7)**
94 Start Understanding The Function Of Graphs
100 **Stop sounding professional (Part 8)**
102 Start Leveraging Pitch, Projection, And Pacing
110 Start Using The Secret 4th P
111 Start Fixing Filler Words
116 **Stop reading slides (Part 9)**
118 Start Doing This Instead
120 **Stop overwriting slides (Part 10)**
122 Start Thinking Of Visual Aides, Not Slides
125 Start Understanding How Your Brain Processes Info
129 Start Designing Slides Like Billboards
139 Start Using The Iceberg Deck
144 **Stop sabotaging concepts (Part 11)**
146 Start Avoiding Concept Juicing
151 Start Saving Storyboards For Directors
156 Start Avoiding Mood Board Blindness

158 Stop talking to yourself (Part 12)
   160   Start Leading Conversations, Not Presentations
   164   Start Asking Better Questions

176 Stop failing your first impression (Part 13)
   178   Start Mastering The First 3 Seconds
   180   Start Opening with the Truth
   183   Start Using Interesting Cover Slides
   187   Start Owning the Spotlight

190 Stop wasting your last impression (Part 14)
   192   Start Replacing Thank You Slides
   196   Start Memorizing

198 Stop believing nerves (Part 15)
   200   Start Understanding Nerves Aren't Real
   204   Start Manipulating The Closed Loop
   205   Start Controlling Your Mind
   208   Start Controlling Your Body

210 Stop standing awkwardly (Part 16)
   212   Start Standing Naturally
   215   Start Playing Simon Says In Meetings
   218   Start Staring Appropriately

220 Stop making virtual meetings harder (Part 17)
   222   Start Controlling Your Lighting
   226   Start Speaking to Camera
   227   Start Owning Your Angles

230 Stop getting stumped (Part 18)
   232   Start Preparing To Improvise
   239   Start Building The Oh Sh*t Toolkit
   242   Start Saying This When You Don't Know The Answer

246 Stop fighting with (or caving to) clients (Part 19)
   248   Start Learning The First Rule of Client Fight Club
   252   Start Abolishing The Myth Of The Dumb Client
   255   Start Handling Objections Confidently

268 Stop taking objections at face value (Part 20)
   270   Start Recognizing 50 Phrases That Kill Creativity
   287   Start Taking "Yes" For An Answer
   288   Start Recognizing The Limits Of Meetings

290 Stop expecting too much from yourself (Part 21)
   292   Start Being Like Bruce Lee
   296   Start Recognizing You Can't Win 'em All
   297   Start Recognizing The Best Part

299 Acknowledgements

FOREWORD

A little less than one score and a few years ago, when I was a junior writer at a renowned Minneapolis agency, the Creative department was given a presentation on how to present. The presenter of this presentation was charisma in carbon form. As if Tony Robbins and Moses had a baby. A baby who was here to present our Lee Jeans scripts.

I left the session somewhat awestruck and with two prevailing feelings. First, that the man possessed some sort of voodoo magic. And second, that would never be me. I can't confirm the first, but I can say for a fact that the second one holds true.

I will never learn to be that kind of presenter. But the good news is I don't have to be. And the good news for every other non-natural-born presentation killer who just wants to present and produce the work you love is that you don't have to be either.

This book is for us.

This book Ben has written and the book you hold in your hands, or the preview of the book you have in your hands as you decide if you should buy it- and by the way, yes you should, it's like what $29, and- wait, what were we talking about? Oh yeah, this is why I need this book.

Stop Reading Slides is full of practical, tangible methods and practices to help you become a comfortable, confident, powerful persuader. In a way that will feel natural and true to you. This book is written by a creative, for creatives. An insider's guide to stepping outside your head in order to present your work in the way it deserves to be seen.

If part of you cringes at the idea of "selling" and another part of you constantly mourns the loss of your best ideas simply because the client doesn't get them, this book is for both parts.

But don't read this book just for you. Read it for all of us. Because the world doesn't need to see your "safe one" or the hardly recognizable compromised version of your once pure and brilliant idea. The world needs to see your best.

This book is about getting your clients to go with your best.

Greg Hahn
Co-Founder & CCO of Mischief USA

INTRODUCTION

I AM NOT A NATURAL PRESENTER

"You can be a little more excited about the work."

I don't remember exactly how many times my CD said this to me coming out of a creative pitch. I know it was more than once. I also know I was confused.

How could I be more excited about the work? Was it a volume issue? Maybe it was a volume issue.

So I talked louder.

STRANGELY ENOUGH, PRESENTING LIKE THIS FOR THE NEXT SIX MONTHS DID NOT SEEM TO HELP.

And that's the problem. It's not enough to know what you're doing wrong. You need to know what to do instead.

We've all heard that we need to use active listening. That we shouldn't say "Um". That we shouldn't read slides.

But no one tells us what to do instead.

It took me five years to figure out the answers to those questions. Five years of experimenting and failing and watching ideas die and hoping my career wasn't about to follow.

You don't have five years. And you don't need them. Because you have this book.

It's about all the things we kinda-sorta know we shouldn't be doing in meetings. And, critically, it's about everything we should start doing instead.

BECAUSE NO ONE SHOULD HAVE TO TALK LIKE THIS TO THEIR CLIENTS FOR SIX MONTHS.

…and no clients should have to hear that either.

STOP BELIEVING IDEAS SELL THEMSELVES

It's not the best ideas that win. It's the most persuasive argument.

I wish it was different. I wish we lived in a world where the best ideas won, where ice cream was an essential part of a six-pack-inducing diet, and where receding hairlines were considered sexy.

But we don't.

Some people get angry when I talk about this. They think I'm saying the creative doesn't matter. But that's not it at all.

Of course creative matters. It just doesn't sell itself.

And the truth is evident to anyone who's ever worked in this industry for longer than five seconds.

How many times have you seen the client choose the "safe" idea?

How many times have you seen derivative work get made, instead of the truly unique concepts?

How many times have you seen brilliant campaigns suffer death by a thousand cuts until they don't resemble the original idea in any way, shape, or form?

But this isn't just my opinion, or even the evidence of my own eyes. It's easily explained with simple psychology.

START
RECOGNIZING WHY CLIENTS BUY BAD IDEAS

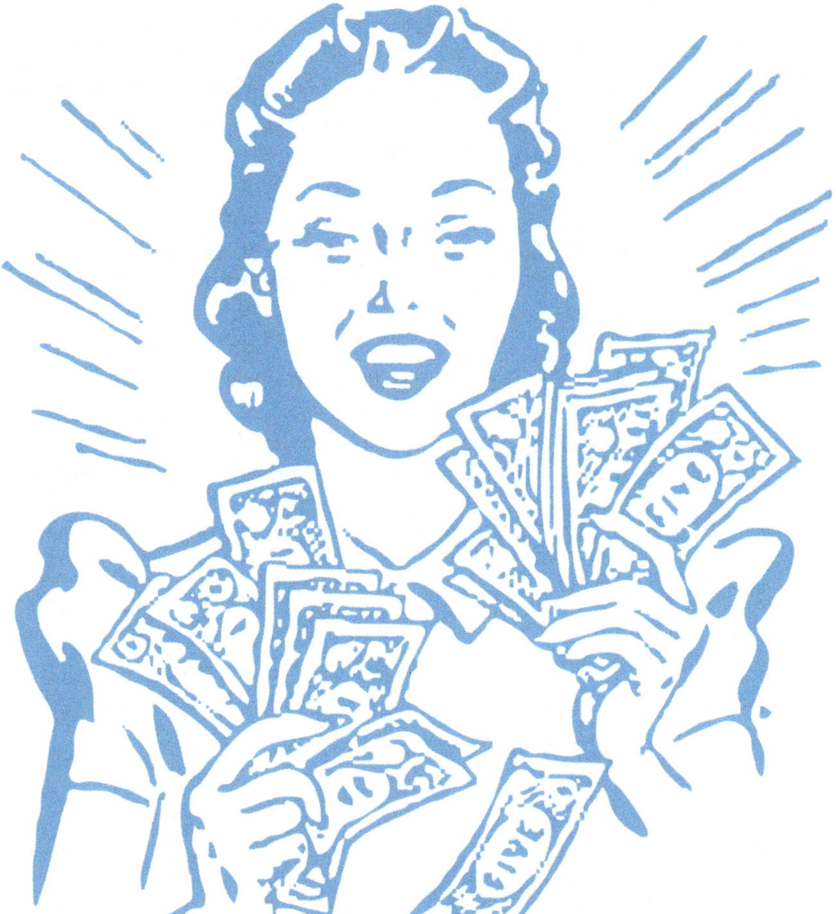

START RECOGNIZING WHY CLIENTS BUY BAD IDEAS

Clients buy bad ideas because they can *understand* them.

Agencies and the people who work in them are advertising experts. And that's a problem. Because if you can't communicate expertise effectively, it comes off as insanity.

This isn't just an agency issue. Galileo was imprisoned in the late seventeenth century for saying that the Earth revolved around the sun. As strong a proof point as any that being right does not mean you'll win.

To put it another way: *You're only as smart as they can understand you to be.*

If you walk in with something truly new, it's difficult for them to wrap their heads around it. Whereas a repeat of the banner campaign they ran last year is a very easy thing for them to envision and feels far less risky by comparison.

STOP BELIEVING IDEAS SELL THEMSELVES

So, it's not just your imagination. Clients do tend to pick the worst (i.e., most common or familiar) idea presented.

The trick is to figure out how to convince them that NOT picking something unique and difficult is — as we all know — the far riskier choice.

Editor's note:

I'm going to use the words "presentation" and "pitch" interchangeably. The lessons in this book apply to any meeting in which you have to persuade someone of something, from a fancy new business meeting to a 15-minute conversation internally.

STOP USING TEMPLATES

I once heard an Account Manager proudly declare that they had the first thirty slides of a deck finished already.

What was weird is we were literally still in the project briefing when they said it.

I mean, it's not impossible.

Maybe they'd gotten a preview of the project from strategy, and had gotten a jump on putting something together? Perhaps they had a history with the brand, and were able to leverage past experiences? Maybe they were just psychic?

Sadly, none of those were correct. Turns out they had just grabbed the agency template, which consisted of thirty pages of boilerplate fluff, changed the client logo on the cover slide, and were trying to pass this off as a job well-started.

It's natural to want to do this. It feels like progress. But it's actually the presentational equivalent of arranging deck chairs on the Titanic.

So here's what you should do instead.

START THINKING OF PRESENTATIONS AS ADS

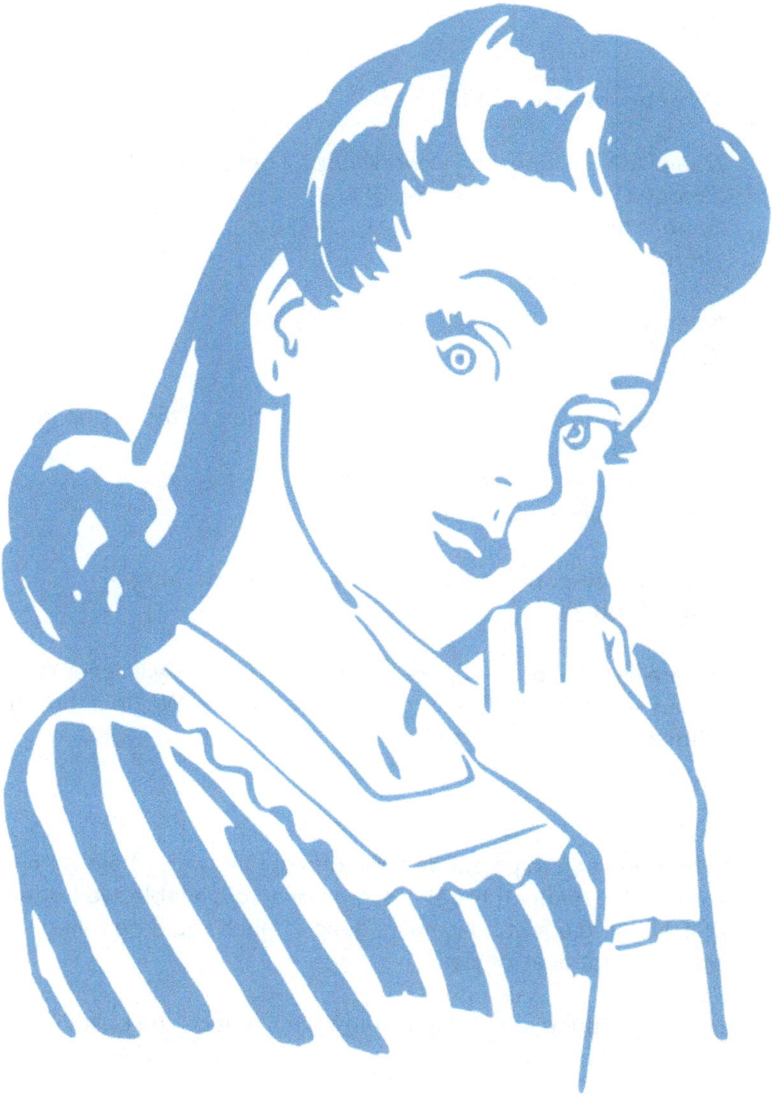

"What makes a good ad?"

When I ask this question in workshops, I get answers like:
"Emotion"
"Simplicity"
"Story"
"Excitement"
"Interest"
"Clarity"

And these are all true. You probably had most of those pop into your head before you even read them.

Why am I talking about ads?

The purpose of an ad is to convince someone to buy something. So is the purpose of a pitch.

We are literal experts at persuading strangers we will never meet to part with their money for goods and services. We do it through billboards, videos, and activations.

And yet…

When we need to persuade a handful of folks with whom we have a relationship, either through a screen or across a table, we forget all of it. Nothing about how most agencies pitch could be called simple, emotional, or clear.

In short, nothing about the average pitch reflects the best advertising practices.

This is actually great news. It means you have all the skills necessary to persuade people to buy your ideas. You just need to start applying them to a "new" medium: the presentation.

STOP USING TEMPLATES

START ABANDONING TEMPLATES

On the next page, I'm going to show you what your presentation decks look like.

I shouldn't be able to do this, of course. There are a lot of people on Earth [citation needed] and a lot of agencies [citation needed].

So the odds are we've never met or worked together before. I've probably never seen one of your decks.

But I'm going to do it anyway. And I feel completely confident in my ability to do so. Ready?

Abra Kadabra, Alakazam:

EVERY AGENCY DECK

Title slide
Table of contents
Agency intros
Case studies
Brand promise
Problem
Audience
Insight
Brief
Creative
Media
Timing
Costs
Thank you slide
Appendix I-IX

How'd I do?

In every workshop I've ever given, the response to this list is uncomfortable silence, nods, and someone saying quietly "Ouch."

The trouble with this is that it's not a story.

What it is, is a chronological checklist of how the sausage gets made.

STOP USING TEMPLATES

The project came in, so it needed a name (Title slide)
We had to figure out what was needed (Table of contents)
We had to assign folks to it (Agency intros)
Yada, yada, yada.

It's a boring, overly detailed timeline of all your work to get here.

Nothing about this makes a story. It barely even includes the client in the narrative. It's just about showing all the effort *you* made.

And it's become a pervasive, predictable habit. A knee-jerk reaction to a meeting appearing on our calendars. A completely anticipated approach from every agency trying to sell itself as unique.

I do have good news, though.

The better, more persuasive way to present is much simpler than that terrible template.

It just requires you to answer four questions.

Here they are.

START
USING THE STORY THAT ALWAYS WINS

This is not about a hero's journey or a beginning, middle, and end. It's about answering four questions.

That's right. Four magic questions.

I've never seen an idea sold that didn't answer these four things for the client.

Often without realizing it. Almost always with a ton of wasted space and slide bloat in between.

But if you answer these questions, in this order, you will increase clarity, simplify your process, and create a single, compelling story for your presentation almost without trying.

STOP USING TEMPLATES

HOW THE WORLD IS
(CONTEXT)

Something about the world today is unsatisfactory. We know this because otherwise your client/prospect would not be spending time and money on a meeting.

The problem could be that they're dead last in their category.

It could also be that they're on top of the world. The category leader. The undisputed king of their domain. But now they have no idea what to do to stay there. (It's a great problem, but it's still a problem.)

This context could come through insights about culture, challenges your client faces, or opportunities that exist but are not being taken advantage of. And it should register emotionally.

You'll know you did this right when they become visibly uncomfortable.

> **Facepalm for the win**
>
> I was freelancing on a pitch for a fitness chain. They had made the unusual decision to stay open throughout the COVID-19 pandemic, and as a result their numbers had swelled. But in late 2022 restrictions were easing, and the chain needed to figure out what to do next.
>
> This was how I opened the pitch:
>
> *"Your numbers have been great because, for the last two years, you've had a competitive advantage.*
>
> *But as the world starts to inch back to 'normal,' you need a message more compelling than 'Our doors are unlocked.'"*
>
> At which point the president of the chain hid his face in his hands and said, *"Jesus, Ben!"*
>
> I waited until he looked me in the eyes again. *"Am I wrong?"*

You want them to feel this level of discomfort. Because once they do, it's no longer just a meeting to hear about an opportunity. It's a meeting about a critical problem that they want to go away. It becomes urgent. It becomes important.

And to be clear, it's real. I'm not manufacturing this level of drama (Well, ok, that example was dramatic. I'm not always that blunt. But I knew the client well enough to know they needed a shock).

The point is to put a stake in the ground (or in their hearts) and make them feel the importance of the moment. This isn't their only meeting of the day. You need them focused.

STOP USING TEMPLATES

HOW THE WORLD COULD BE (DREAM)

This is their vision of a better tomorrow. A world where the issues plaguing your client no longer exist. Their personal Valhalla. Their Promised Land. The answer to all the pain you just made them feel a moment ago.

Spoiler Alert: This will not be *"You could get a ten percent increase in clickthrough rate (CTR) per month."*

Your goal is to make this as visceral and real to them as their problems do. Paint this picture for your audience- talk to them about how it will impact their consumers, their business, and the world as it is today.

Make them feel this as fully as they did the previous answer.

How the World Could Be:

You could own 100% of a media buy that doesn't exist yet.
or
Your banners could become a whole new genre of entertainment.

Would either of the above answer the need to increase CTR by ten percent? Yes. But they do it in a way that gives your clients something to root for. To dream of.

If they're at the bottom of their category, simply saying, *"You'll be at the top!"* isn't enough. Just like *How the World Is* needs to make them feel what they might intellectually know, *How the World Could Be* needs to make them taste the benefits of an objective goal.

Talk about the changes that will occur in consumer behavior. The rise in brand reputation. The increased respect of their peers.

Do this right, and an incredible thing happens: they want your ideas to work before they even hear them.

It makes sense. A minute ago you made them hurt. Now you're promising that the pain won't just end; they'll get a cool-looking Band-Aid and a lollipop and stickers to go with it. They want this to be true.

STOP USING TEMPLATES

If you get the answers to these first two questions right, they will love you before seeing a single piece of work.

BUT.

How the World Could Be is the step we most often miss.

Just about every agency will outline the client's problem in some form. But then almost all of us immediately jump to the solution. *Without telling the client why they want it.*

We're so excited to get to the work, we forget to tell our audience about the benefits. And that's understandable. We've spent hours/days/weeks thinking about the work. To us, it's obvious why our ideas are the solution to the problems.

But let me put this in the context of an ad again.

We tell our clients all the time that they can't promote the features, they need to push the benefits. *"Sell the sizzle, not the steak,"* as the saying goes.

Our work is the steak. The benefits are the sizzle. Most agencies fail to realize this. But the harsh truth is:

The client isn't paying you for the work. They don't actually care about the work. They care about what the work does for them.

So hit this hard. And if you do it right, they'll be rooting for your ideas before they even know what they are.

HOW YOU'RE GONNA MAKE IT HAPPEN (WORK)

If they've agreed with your assessment of the world today, and have been inspired by your vision of the world as it could be, then the next logical question is *"But how do we make it happen?"* Or in some cases, *"Is what you promise even possible?"*

This is where you show your work.

Now is the time to share your ideas, how you'll make them real, and how much they'll cost.

On the one hand, this is usually the part of the presentation that creative folk feel the most comfortable delivering.

On the other hand, at least half of this book is dedicated to the ways in which we sabotage ourselves in the process.

But before we get lost in those weeds, let's talk about the final question your pitch should answer.

STOP USING TEMPLATES

HOW THE WORLD WILL BE (DREAM AGAIN)

Fun fact: originally, there were only three questions.

But when they finished answering *How You'll Make It Happen*, my clients made the same mistake over and over (and over) again.

Because of the tendency to run through the presentation chronologically, they all finished the same way: by talking about timing, media, and costs.

The three most friction-filled parts of any presentation.

So that was their client's last impression. That this would be costly, complicated, and a lot of work.

It's no wonder most meetings these days end with *"Thanks, we'll gather our thoughts and get back to you".*

So finish with the dream. Remind them that all that money, all that effort, will be for the thing they *really* want. That last impression alone can turn a meeting from *"You've got to be kidding me"* to *"We're gonna have to talk about how we afford this, but we're onboard."*

Multiple times I've watched the work die as the business was won. All because we perfectly articulated the client's vision. It usually shows up in a statement like, "You haven't nailed it yet, but you get us."

People often ask what the difference is between *How the World Could Be* and *How the World Will Be*. And the answer is "not much." Its main purpose is to ensure the pitch ends with the benefit to the client.

I do tend to keep it shorter than *How the World Could Be*, since we've already gotten into it once. It can be as short as a single sentence, if you like. But it needs to be there. Or you'll leave the room with your audience thinking about all the reasons they shouldn't approve your work.

STOP USING TEMPLATES

And there it is. The four questions every successful pitch answers. Four questions that make a story almost without trying.

Simple, right?

| HOW THE WORLD IS | HOW THE WORLD COULD BE | HOW YOU'LL MAKE IT HAPPEN | HOW THE WORLD WILL BE |

START EDITING

Please note that this flow doesn't prevent you from bloating your deck. Don't trick yourself into believing the entirety of Wikipedia is necessary context for *How The World Is*.

"YOUR GOAL IS TO ANSWER THESE QUESTIONS AS CONCISELY AS POSSIBLE!"

Remember, I want you to treat the presentation the same way you would any creative product.

Edit your deck as ruthlessly as you edit your videos. Don't tolerate redundancy, boredom, or a dip in energy.

The length of each answer is dictated by the minimum amount your audience needs to know.

Put differently, I want you to prioritize being compelling over being complete.

STOP USING TEMPLATES

START SELLING LIKE A MINIMALIST

There's this thing I do a lot with clients. I don't do it to be mean, but I worry it can come off that way.

They'll run through their presentation— maybe it's five minutes long, maybe it's an hour— and then I recap it back to them in four-to-six sentences.

After only hearing it once. Without slides.

It's not a magic trick. I know what the four critical questions are that you need to answer in any presentation (just like you do now). And so, I'm mentally highlighting them as I listen.

I'm also a trained copywriter and I do this coaching thing for a living, so I've had a little bit of practice.

But I want you to understand that it's not impossible to do this. That when we talk about editing ruthlessly, that means you could literally get those four questions answered in four Tweets. Without slides.

Let me give you an example.

Example: Heinz IMDB

I have no idea how Rethink sold this work. It could be they just called up the client and said *"We're making you an IMDB page."*

But this is how I'd have done it in four-to-six sentences.

How The World Is
"Heinz Ketchup has been around longer than Coca-Cola. And yet, somehow, they're an icon and you're just a condiment."

How The World Could Be
"It's time we remind everyone that Heinz is the original burger buddy. So you get the iconic, superstar credit you deserve."

How We'll Make It Happen
"So we'll set up an IMDB page for Heinz Ketchup, and call out the hundreds of movies and TV scenes where our iconic bottle went uncredited."

How The World Will Be
"Overnight, you'll become the most credited star in history. The entire world will realize when they sit down to a table with Heinz, they're dining with a celebrity."

Six sentences. Of course for the meeting I'd elaborate on the idea further: remind them that they'll get credit from *Seinfeld*'s diner scenes to *Pulp Fiction*'s briefcase moment to *When Harry Met Sally*'s "I'll have what she's having."

I'd explain how fans will be asked to tag each occurrence, which will give us organic engagement and growth. I'd also probably include some details about public relations opportunities.

STOP USING TEMPLATES

But the first two questions? I'd likely answer them just as I did in this example because the client knows how old they are, and they know their reputation is not on par with Coke's.

I don't need to talk about research, target markets, who we are as an agency, or the site visits that IMDB gets on a daily basis. None of it is essential to making them feel the pain of *How the World Is*, so I'd leave it out.

Similarly, they know what it means to be Coca-Cola. It's the dream of every consumer product goods brand. I don't need to beat them over the head with that hope, either. I say just enough to make them start dreaming.

Wait for it

I was told an apocryphal story about the first meeting between Domino's and their agency CP+B.

The agency opens the meeting with, *"Your pizza isn't very good."*

Offended, the Domino's team pushes back their chairs and gets up to leave.

"Wait, wait," says CP+B, *"Burger King doesn't make great burgers. You can be the Burger King of pizza."*

At which point Domino's sits back down.

How the World Is and How the World Could Be in three lines.

PRACTICE EXERCISE: PITCHING CASE STUDIES

What you'll need:

A case study of work. It doesn't have to be yours. Steal something you love from the award shows this past year.

What you'll do:

Watch the case study. Then try to imagine how you would pitch it using the four questions.

It may take you a few tries to get your answers as tight as the previous examples, but the more you do it, the easier it will become.

Why a case study? Good case studies condense and highlight the relevant information around the problem *(How the World Is)* the goal (How it Could Be) the work *(How You'll Make It Happen)* and the result *(How It Will Be)*.

So, it'll be easier for you to identify these parts by watching a case study as opposed to manufacturing them out of thin air based on the execution alone.

Bonus:

Do the exercise above, but then record yourself pitching it. Don't worry about any slides for now, just see how the language feels and how smooth (or not) your transitions are from one question to another.

STOP USING TEMPLATES

PRESENTING
THE PITCH PYRAMID
A GEOMETRICALLY PLEASING WAY TO KEEP YOUR PITCH PROGRESSING PROPERLY.

I'm not saying you have to scan this, print it out, assemble it, and put it on your desk. I'm just saying that if you do, you have to send me a photo.

START LEVERAGING THE INVISIBLE BRIEF

At this point, people often like to ask me how I know the right answers to the four questions. After all, there are a hundred different ways you could describe *How the World Is*. So, how do you pick?

Enter the *Invisible Brief*.

STOP USING TEMPLATES

If a pitch or presentation is a form of advertising, then it stands to reason it should have its own creative brief.

…I'd like to ask all the planners to step away from the torches and pitchforks for a moment.

I'm not suggesting you write a brief for your meeting. But I do want to point out something very, very important:

You are not pitching your campaign's target.

No one has ever been briefed to convince a company's CMO to buy more of its products or services.

It's never happened.

This is why- after you spend hours, days, and weeks finding the perfect way to reach a target audience- the person you're pitching that idea to often doesn't get it.

It's not for them.

The target might be tweens in middle-income families with a little extra pocket money and a sweet tooth. But in the meeting you're pitching the perfect influencer for that audience to a table full of older men who each own two vacation homes and a modestly sized yacht.

So- after you've come up with the perfect solution for the visible brief- you need to consider what it is that will motivate the people you're seeking approval from.

Luckily, humans are pretty easy to understand.

START ASKING WHAT'S THEIR MOTIVATION?

In my opinion, people are motivated by three things:
- Money
- Power
- Fame

And correctly identifying which one motivates your audience will help you persuade them to buy the best work. Also, you don't need to hire a private investigator to figure out what makes them tick.

Let's take it from the bottom.

Fame
This one is easy to identify. If your client counterpart (or agency boss) is always talking about winning awards, they're motivated by fame. If they're always ranting about how so-and-so got their quote in *The Drum* or *Times* or *Harvard Business Review*, they're motivated by fame.

For clients like these, make sure to include a few mock headlines or potential award categories they could enter when you cover *How the World Could Be/Will be*.

Power
This is someone who wants to be in charge. They constantly complain about how they'd *"change things around here"* or *"how stupid everyone else"* in the organization is. They want the corner office, and it's your job to make them recognize that your ideas are an essential ingredient in getting it.

This is the kind of person who often won't let you present your own ideas up the ladder, because they jealously guard face time with the big boss. So, talk about how you'll make them a deck or whatever pretty charts are required to take all the glory. Instead of praise, you'll have to be satisfied with getting your best ideas made.

STOP USING TEMPLATES

Money

I was talking about the Invisible Brief to an Executive Creative Director once, and he got excited and told me I'd just reframed an entire relationship for him. Here's the story in his words:

Creative value

"I was on production with a client, and we went to dinner. He told me his annual bonus paid for his kids' private school. In that moment I realized he'll always be motivated by the money."

This ECD recognized he couldn't do anything to jeopardize his client's bonus.

Therefore, his goal was to explain how– no matter what happens– the work being presented won't risk those end-of-the-year numbers.

With that in mind, he could walk in with an argument like:

"I know this is a different approach for us, but we're only using five percent of the budget to start. Think of it as a test run.

If it doesn't work, our traditional campaign will perform like it traditionally does. If this different approach does work, the year will look even better than expected, and next year we can go big with it."

START LOOKING BEHIND THE NUMBERS

At this point, some folks will be shouting, *"But my client loves numbers!"*

Of course they do. But they love those numbers because they're the secret to getting more money, power, or fame. No one wants numbers for the sake of numbers. So please don't think your client is driven by data. They're driven by how they intend to use that data.

START ASKING WHAT ARE THEIR VALUES?

Money, power, and fame aren't the only ways to understand a client. You can also look at their values when trying to answer the four questions.

Do they serve:
- The company
- The customer
- Themselves

This time, we'll take it from the top.

The Company
These folks are easy to identify, because they're always wearing the three-quarter zip fleece with the company logo emblazoned on the chest. They wear it to every video call. On every production. They probably keep a second one to wear when the first one's in the wash. I'm just kidding. It's much more likely they shower in it.

A client like this loves the company with all their heart. They never want to work anywhere else. They hope to be buried in a branded coffin out in the parking lot.

And you can talk to them using words like "brand" and "legacy" because they wholeheartedly think in those terms.

The Customer
This is someone who truly believes that their job makes a difference to society. I'll give you an example from my own career.

STOP USING TEMPLATES

> **One Note**
>
> As a young writer I got to work on a new running shoe launch for New Balance.
>
> Our client shared early on that he had just left Nike after fifteen years owing to an argument with higher-ups about the direction the company was heading.
>
> He'd been told that skate and basketball shoes would take precedence over running shoes — that's where the profit was for the company.
>
> As a result, he'd gone to New Balance because, in his words, *"They make the best running shoes these days."*

Message received: this guy is all about the runners.

And so we didn't just talk about the retailers, but about what this new launch would do for the folks who actually lace up their shoes at six a.m. in the rain.

Over the course of a full launch campaign that included a direct mail kit, custom swag, a microsite, and a mini-documentary, he only ever gave us one note.

He asked us to cut the documentary about 30 seconds shorter.

That was it.

That's the power of understanding how to talk to your client about your work.

Themselves

Not everyone answers to a higher purpose. For many, their job is a means to an end. They clock in, clock out, and that's it. There's nothing wrong with that. But, you can't talk to someone like this about brand legacy or the greater good. They'll laugh you out of the room.

If you find yourself presenting to someone like this, your best bet is to refer to the list of motivations.

START
GETTING CLEAR
ON THE POINT

One of the final things you should consider when answering the *Invisible Brief* is, *"Exactly what do we need coming out of the meeting?"*

Most people will tell you the point of the meeting is to get the work approved.

[incorrect buzzer sounds]

The ultimate goal is to get the work approved, sure. But that's way too broad for all but the final meeting. Think smaller:

The point of every meeting is to get to the next one.

A ton of arguments, confusion, and objections occur because we fail to recognize this fact. We turn the deck into a Swiss-Army Knife of contingencies and discussions for things that are only going to become relevant weeks from now.

And this breaks our clients' brains.

START
RUNNING MEETINGS
ONE GOAL AT A TIME

Consider for a moment a meeting where the client asks you to present research, strategy, a variety of concepts, and production costs. This is an all-too-common ask as budgets and timelines continue to shrink.

First, you present the research. Maybe you pause for their approval, maybe you don't. But you need their approval of your findings either way, at least implicitly.

STOP USING TEMPLATES

That approval is followed by the brief, which also needs to be approved.

I hope that wasn't a problem, because now they need to choose between three campaigns built on those previous two approvals.

Assuming you've approved at least one of the campaigns (three approvals down, for those keeping score) you now just have to get the budget and timeline approved.

With every one of these cascading implications, your audience's blood pressure will rise. With every approval being sought, you ratchet up the tension and the stakes. They are quite literally being asked to make massive decisions every few minutes throughout the meeting.

They'll respond by shutting down. This is another reason why so many meetings end with "We have to go back and think about it." You've broken your audience.

If the client tries to ask for cascading deliverables in a meeting, try pushing back. Tell them that you're worried about wasting their time and money on the campaigns without the necessary steps (like strategy) approved first.

Explain that rather than present everything in ninety minutes a month from now, you'd like to have weekly thirty-minute meetings focused on each separate approval.

As much as possible, boil down the process until you can identify the single next approval you need, and then focus on getting that.

It won't always work. But when it does, every meeting will go smoother. Plus, you'll know how to weigh the four answers to your presentation.

START
ASKING WHY ARE WE MEETING (THIS TIME)?

What's the client looking for next? Is it strategy? Creative? The delivery plan? It's essential to know.

Because these four questions are not simply the four quarters of your presentation.

Remember that your goal is to answer them as succinctly as possible. Which means that the amount of time you devote to each section will change depending on the purpose of that meeting.

For example, let's say you've made it through the RFP (request-for-proposal) process and get a first meeting with a potential new client. Your presentation will probably look like this:

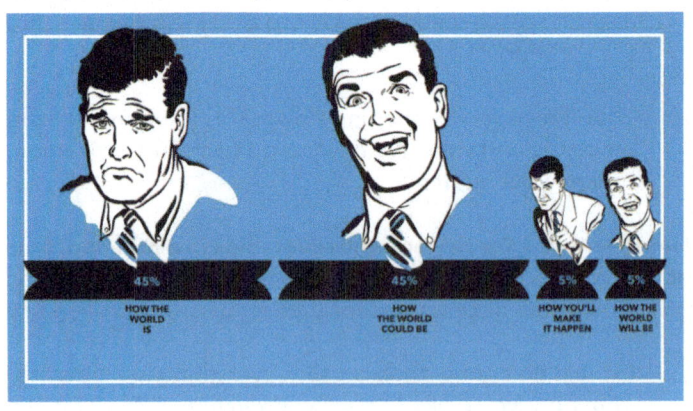

45%	45%	5%	5%
HOW THE WORLD IS	HOW THE WORLD COULD BE	HOW YOU'LL MAKE IT HAPPEN	HOW THE WORLD WILL BE

(Those percentages represent presentation minutes, not number of slides.)

Most of your time will be spent talking to them about what challenges they're facing and what the potential upside could be of working together.

Then, maybe you pull out a few case studies to show you have the skills to back up your swagger. And, of course, you end the presentation by reminding them just how awesome the world could be if you join forces. But you're spending most of your time on those first two questions.

STOP USING TEMPLATES

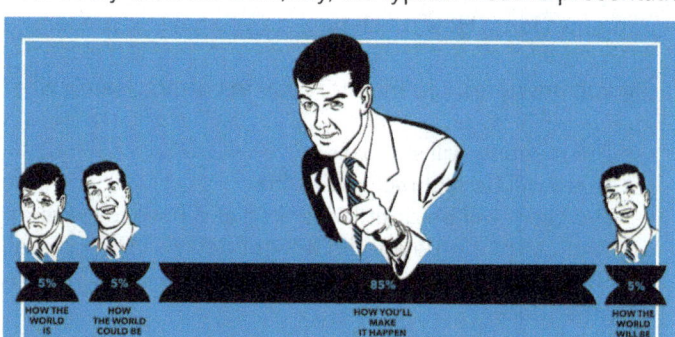

That's very different from, say, the typical creative presentation:

(Again: we're talking minutes, not pages.)

Here, we're just briefly touching on the context and dream. After all, we've covered those in previous meetings. We don't want anyone to forget them, but we don't need to re-introduce the brief, the team, or any of that again.

Which is why most of the time is going to be spent on the work. With just a minute or two left over to remind them what all that work is for.

Don't fall into the trap of believing these answers get equal billing in every meeting. In fact, if you start to feel like they need to be equal, it's usually a red flag that too much is being asked for all at once.

When you look at how you're breaking up the four questions or how much content you have for a meeting, you're looking at minutes. Not page count. So, if you're committing five percent of your time to *How The World Is*, that means whoever's leading the charge there has three minutes. You can pack a hundred slides into that if you're interested in making it a flipbook. Just know that if you're not done in three minutes, I'm coming for you with an oversized shepherd's crook like a bad Vaudeville act.

Oh, and speaking of time…

START PLANNING FOR ½ TIME

Pop quiz, hotshot: You've got a meeting with the client. It's 60 minutes long. How much time do you have to present?

If you answered "30 minutes" you're correct. Here's why:

- The meeting will start late
- There will be technical difficulties
- The client will be double-booked and have to leave early
- Your car/plane/palanquin will get delayed/stuck in traffic/lost
- The meeting will contain extra attendees having to present other decks
- The fire alarm will go off
- You'll spend 15 minutes discussing that super hot new show everyone's watching
- It will take longer to go through the work than you thought
- You'll actually build a rapport with your client and spend thirty minutes talking, without slides, about the thing you're in the room to talk about.

All of these have happened to me at least once.

And if you plan to only fill half your allotted time, you'll be ready for any of it.

So if you have a 60-minute meeting, make sure you can get through your slides (at a normal speaking pace) in 30 minutes.

30-minute meeting? You've got 15 minutes.

15-minute meeting? This is probably just a phone call to cover one single point. Anything more than that is gonna be a disaster.

STOP USING TEMPLATES

When I talk about *1/2 Time*, people usually have two concerns. Excuses. Reasons For Trepidation.

Reason One: Eager to Please
We put too much crap into the meeting because we assume more content equals more satisfied client. Stop doing that. The new rule is you cannot put sixty minutes of deck into a sixty-minute meeting. Thirty minutes max.

Violators will be replaced with bobbleheads. Because at least then their contributions won't have a negative impact on the meeting.

Reason Two: "But the Clients Paid for a Full Hour!"
A presentation is not a Broadway show. No one gets upset if it ends early. In fact, they love you for it.

You have given them more time for lunch. More time to catch up on emails. Hell, they can just sit around and watch cat videos for a bit if that's what'll make them happy.

Don't worry about ending early. Worry about having to rush through the session, leaving no time for a relationship-building discussion, and forcing your client to default to "let us discuss, and we'll get back to you."

Example: Boost Mobile Fairy Tales

The best way to demonstrate this is through video. But for right now, I'll share the slides and the talk track.

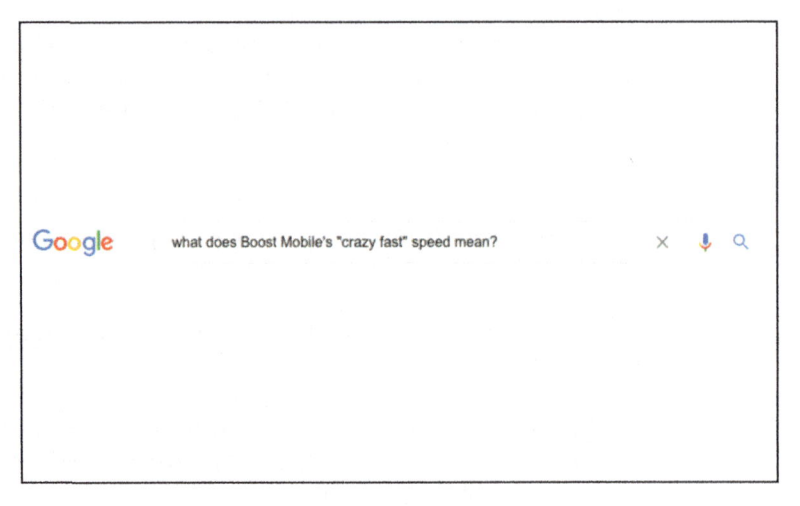

[Google search bar: "what does Boost Mobile's "crazy fast" speed mean?"]

To a room of Boost Mobile marketing folks:

"If you ask the internet what Boost Mobile's tagline means, there's not a single suggested answer. So let me ask- what does "Crazy Fast Speeds" mean to you?"

Uncomfortable silence. Some shifting. One answer. Then another, slightly different one.

"If I asked your spouses that question, would I get the same answer? What about a customer leaving one of your stores in Brooklyn? In Cheboygan?

"Crazy Fast Speeds" doesn't have any meaning to your customers. But we have a chance to change that. All we need is something that's equally familiar to a hipster in Brooklyn and a grandmother in Cheboygan. Something like…"

STOP USING TEMPLATES

"Fairy tales. We all know the stories. Which is why they're the perfect platform for us to show what "Crazy Fast Speeds" can mean to people."

"We'll retell famous fairy tales and use them to show the impact that your network can have in their life."

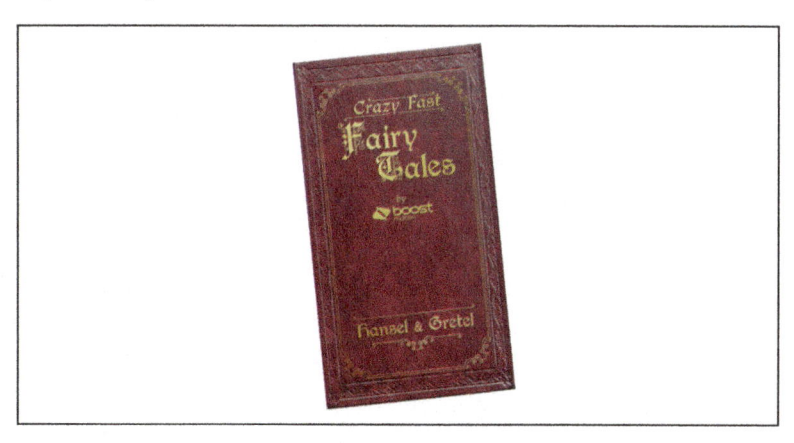

"Introducing *"Crazy Fast Fairy Tales",* by Boost Mobile. A familiar tale in four frames."

HANSEL + GRETEL

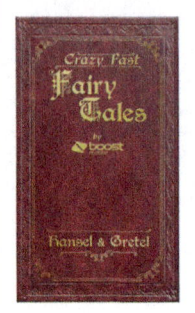

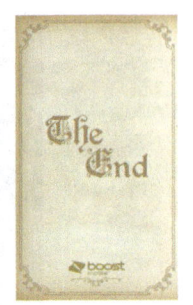

"Hansel and Gretel were lost in a forest, so they used their crazy fast data to find their way home. The end."

OTHER STORIES

The Frog Prince

Frame 1	Frame 2	Frame 3	Frame 4
A book cover "Crazy Fast Fairy Tales by Boost Mobile: The Frog Prince"	A crowned frog "There once was a prince who was turned into a frog."	A Tinder-like match page showing a princess "So he used his Crazy Fast data to find a maiden's kiss."	Interior page with logo "The End"

Humpty Dumpty

Frame 1	Frame 2	Frame 3	Frame 4
A book cover "Crazy Fast Fairy Tales by Boost Mobile: Humpty Dumpty"	A crowned frog "All the King's men couldn't put Humpty together again."	Close up of a phone "Until they used their Crazy Fast data to stream a DIY tutorial."	Interior page with logo "The End"

"And we can repeat this with every benefit we want to discuss, giving meaning and significance to Crazy Fast Speeds four frames at a time."

STOP USING TEMPLATES

"We can run this almost indefinitely. Aside from there being hundreds of stories we can call on; we could even adapt this to modern epic moments – bringing in fairy tale moments in sports and culture as they happen.

Whatever benefits and features we want to highlight, we can do so under the Crazy Fast banner. And when we're done, we won't just have a new campaign. We'll have a comprehensive, clear understanding of what Boost Mobile's Crazy Fast Speeds mean for your customers."

...AND THEY LIVED HAPPILY EVER AFTER.

They bought the campaign, invested triple the budget they had originally proposed, and ran it for a year. Here's why:

How the World Is
Their brief said *"Facebook has new technology with sliding mobile frames. We want to jump on it."* We said, *"You have an empty set of words for a tagline."*

They came with the business brief. We came with the larger pain point. And we proved it with a simple question that the room couldn't answer (You'll notice the brief never made an appearance).

How the World Could Be
Because of that, we turned a meeting about "seeing some ideas" into "solving a massive, brand-wide problem they didn't realize they had". Which, I knew, mattered to our audience because they were high-level CMO types that cared about the larger message of the brand, not just checking the box of a new social feature.

STOP USING TEMPLATES

How We'll Make It Happen
I explained exactly what we were going to do up front – remix fairy tales. I only got into the details afterward. And even then, those details didn't include unnecessary detours into the obvious, like how every one of these will have to be illustrated.

We'll dive into the significance of those choices in future chapters.

How the World Will Be
I ended on the dream. I reminded them that the reason we're going to tell all these silly stories is to give them something worth infinitely more than the effort or cost involved. We would create substance and meaning for an empty set of words they had been using for years.

Of course they said yes.

Seven slides. Around five minutes. And the result was an entirely new campaign for the brand, approved with no notes from the client.

STOP CALLING YOUR CONCEPTS EQUAL

3

This is the part where someone usually says, *"Okay Baldy, sounds great. But what if I'm walking in with more than one idea?"*

Which, aside from the comment on my hair, is a legitimate question.

There are a few things to keep in mind if you're sharing multiple ideas.

First, you will still only have one answer for *How the World Is* and *How the World Will Be*. The problem and the ultimate promise should both be big enough to encompass all the concepts. Second, I shave my head, ok? It's a choice.

START SHARING MULTIPLE IDEAS INTENTIONALLY

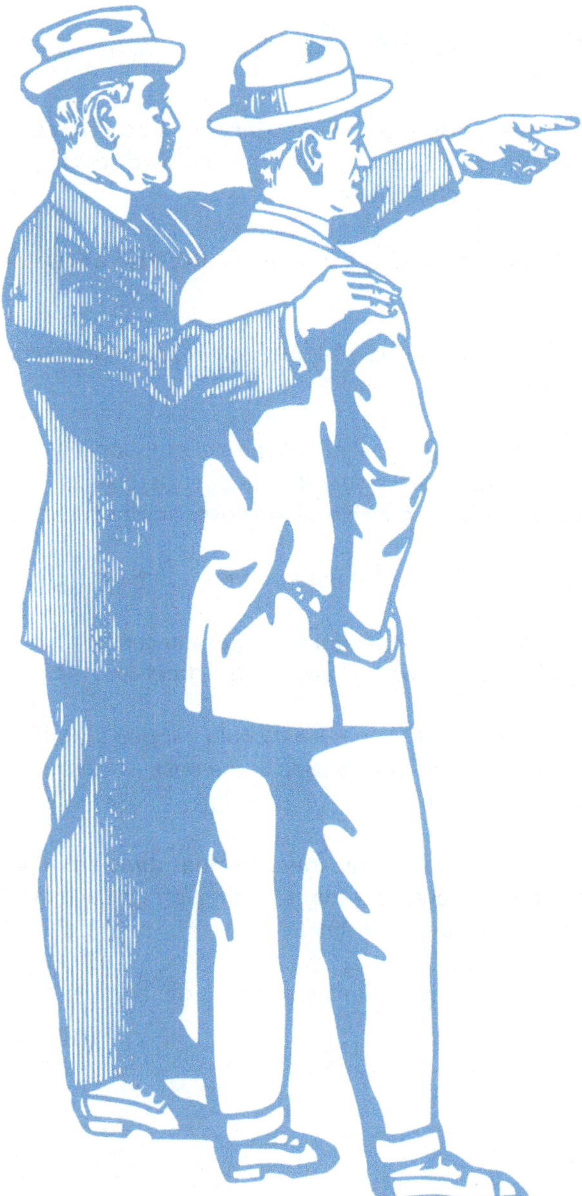

START SHARING MULTIPLE IDEAS PURPOSEFULLY

Don't ever present multiple concepts "because they asked for multiple ideas." Each concept should be distinct in strategy, approach, or execution.

Please do not walk into the meeting and say "Here's idea one... idea two.... and idea three..."

You might as well ask, *"Would you like your campaign in red, blue, or green?"*

Remember, your goal is to generate emotion in your clients and to prove impact. Make sure the client understands the reason why they would want to go with one idea over another:

"Approach A is your standard tone and media.

Approach B is about showing what you can do if, instead of buying TV like you've always done, we use street-level activations.

And Approach C shows what could happen if we took a slightly wittier tone than you've used in the past, while still remaining within the brand voice."

See? Those aren't three ideas to meet some arbitrary quota. Those are three different solutions. Each might still achieve the client's goals, but they are distinct.

Speaking of distinctions, it's time to get brutally honest here.

STOP CALLING YOUR CONCEPTS EQUAL

START TAKING STRAW DOGS BEHIND THE BARN

I don't know where the idea of "Let's present a concept for the client to kill" came from. But it can go right the hell back there. Do not pass GO. Do not collect two hundred dollars.

I don't want to hear about your "safe" concepts "just in case."

I don't want to hear about *"We wanted to show this idea just so they know that we've heard of this new media."* .

You do not show anything you wouldn't want to make. Ever.

Period. End of discussion. No exceptions. I will fight you.

START CHOOSING FAVORITE CHILDREN

I do not love "my children" equally. And neither do you.

This is a critically important part of presenting multiple ideas. You must make a recommendation.

"We love all our ideas equally and think any of them will work for you."

No, you don't. One of those idea babies is your favorite. But just like my Mom, you're too chicken to admit it to my face.

Deny it and I'll know you're lying.

So will your client.

Which is why ending your pitch without a strong recommendation drives me insane.

There are usually two reasons why an agency doesn't want to recommend a direction:

1. "We don't want to appear pushy."
2. "We don't want them to think any of the other work is bad."

I will address both of these concerns using something I know almost nothing about: plumbing.

If you have a leaky pipe, a plumber will come over and probably say something like,

"Well, there's a couple of things we could do. The best thing to do is replace that section of pipe. It'll cost you more, but I promise you'll never see me again for this issue."

I can also patch it. That'll be cheaper, and it'll solve your issue for now. But I can't guarantee it won't leak again one day."

To all the folks who identify with reason one, would that plumber seem pushy to you?

They're just laying out the options clearly. And one is—in their professional opinion—the best. Now, they've given us all the information we need to make a choice.

To all the folks who identify with reason two, do you feel like one of those solutions is bad?

I mean, I get that the first option is the best. But they're not saying the second won't work. It's just not their first choice.

STOP CALLING YOUR CONCEPTS EQUAL

Pretending that all your ideas are equal calls your credibility into question.

Coming in with a strong recommendation shows you're an expert. It demonstrates you've thought through all the possible solutions.

And while they *are* all solutions, they *are not* all equal.

So have a favorite and tell your client what it is and why.

Also? You need to know which one you love best so you can have an agency recommendation. Which you need.

Otherwise, when the client ends the meeting by asking, *"What do you guys recommend?"*, you'll end up doing that thing where everyone looks either open-mouthed or panic-eyed.

Shock and puzzlement are not the last impressions you want to leave.

START CONSIDERING JUST BRINGING ONE

A final thought about presenting multiple ideas. I know some clients insist on seeing options. And if the assignment clearly stated three concepts, you're risking a breach of contract by not delivering three.

But it's worth remembering that occasionally there really is only one right answer to the client's problem. Standing behind your one true solution is a gutsy way of proving that to them. Also, see my earlier point about straw dogs and barns...

STOP TRYING TO MEMORIZE

People sometimes think of presenting as public speaking with slides. But there are massive differences between the two.

If you're giving a talk, you have time to prepare and memorize your content. And you can comfortably assume no one will be interrupting you to ask that you go back three slides.

Agency presentations roll differently.

I've been handed a deck I've never seen before, for a project I'm not part of, and pushed into the room five minutes after the meeting already started.

I've had clients interrupt me on slide two (more on that story later).

You won't have time to memorize. And you won't have the luxury of saying your piece uninterrupted. So I don't want you to memorize an entire hour's worth of words.

Just a few bullets.

START THINKING IN BULLETS

Use a Word doc. Or go old school with pen and paper.

Some people restrict themselves to a single thought per sheet, spreading them out like a slightly less organized conspiracy theorist. Others use sticky notes (awesome when working solo, difficult to read for groups).

However you choose, the point is to find your points.

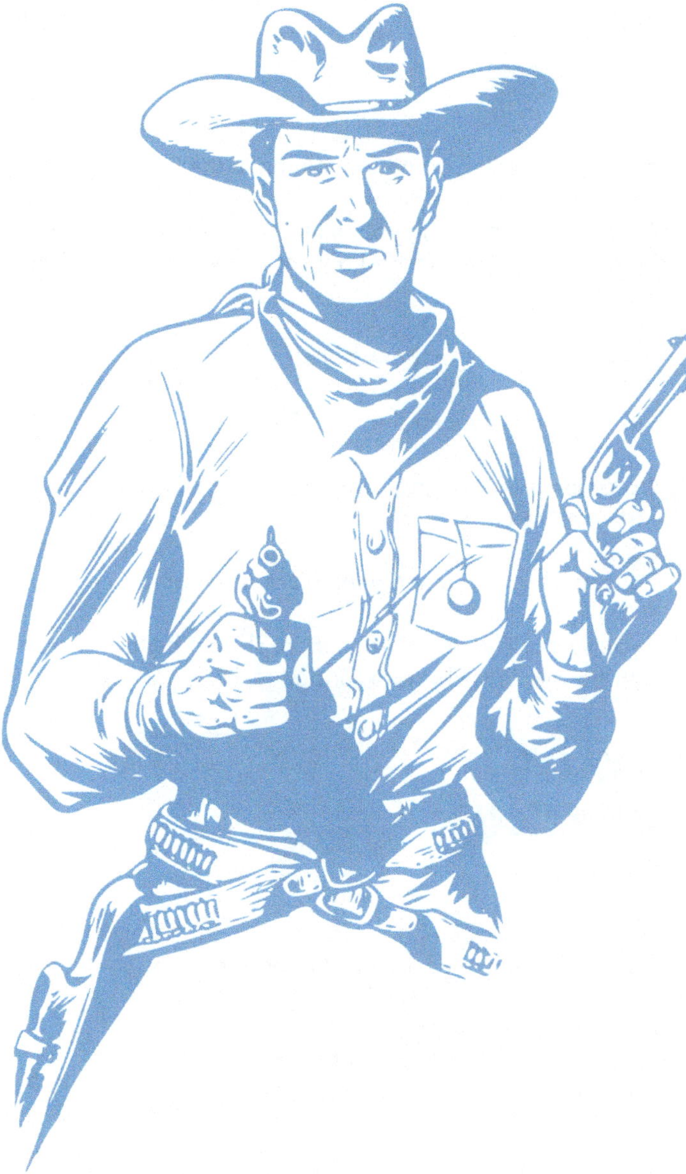

START WITH A MESS

Initially, you're just going for volume in the bullet stage.

Write down everything you think could conceivably be important. Random thoughts. Fleshed out concepts. Rationales. Insights. Everything.

Then, start grouping those bullets under the appropriate question.

Have a point about audience behavior? Put it under *How the World Is*.

A problem you're trying to solve? *How the World Could Be* (once you've solved it).

Concepts? *How You're Gonna Make It Happen*.

If you've done your job right, there should be four giant columns with masses of sticky notes under each.

START ASKING WHY

Now, ask which ones are most important.

Why am I including this?
Why does it support my argument?
Why should the audience care?

As you answer those questions, you'll start creating more bullets, rearranging others, and discarding a bunch. And before you know it, you'll have an outline.

STOP TRYING TO MEMORIZE

START PARING DOWN

Keep in mind your end goal isn't to have more bullets, but fewer.

This isn't about all the reasons the brand's numbers are down. You're looking for a few perfect phrases that will let you stay on target.

A good way to know if you've done this wrong? If your bullets are sentences.

If you've put so much info down that it's a line or two, you've got more editing to do.

Remember my *Crazy Fast* deck? Here are the bullets:

- Crazy Fast =?
- Define and build pride
- Universal reference
- Work
- Endless executions

Notice how those are not slides or sentences. What they are is a cheat sheet so condensed that I can memorize it in three minutes. It is a map I can always return to, much like Hansel's GPS.

See what I did there?

START MEMORIZING BULLETS

Now all you need to remember is a series of bullets.

Not your slides. Not a "perfect" script you've planned out in your mind. Just the bullets.

And since all you need to remember are bullets, you'll be able to run through the entire presentation quickly. Five, ten minutes, tops.

Which means you don't need to book a conference room and go through your slides front to back once an hour.

You're going to be running through them five times in the shower. Three times in the elevator. And during lunch. With plenty of time to spare for a tuna fish sandwich. With a side of chips. Damn it, I'm hungry now.

The point is, if you have the bullets, you won't lose the plot. Or, even if you do (like I just did), you'll know exactly where to pick up from and continue naturally.

STOP TRYING TO MEMORIZE

START USING SLIDES AS NOTES

Let's talk about notes for a second. When I talk about bullets and prepping slides and memorization, someone always asks about notes.

I don't use notes. Ever. Doesn't matter if it's a two-hour meeting. There are no notes.

> In fact, I've given lectures for five hours a day, for four days straight, and never used a single note. And my mutant power is most definitely not memorization. It's sweating.
>
> TMI, I know.
>
> There are, of course, things I need to repeat verbatim to my audience. Sometimes they're statistics. Or famous quotes. Or even a specific question I want to pose to the room.
>
> But I don't memorize any of it. I put it right on the slide.

Think about it- if something is so important you can't afford to forget it, it's worth sharing with the whole class.

> We'll expand on this in a bit, but the short version is this: my slides ARE my notes.
>
> I read them at the same time everyone else does.
>
> Go back and check out that *Crazy Fast* example. You'll see that even the slides with little or no words on them are still visual mnemonics for the thoughts I wanted to share.

START TRUSTING YOURSELF

Inevitably, when I talk about this, folks panic. They worry that without a script, or more complete notes, they'll forget things.

But we're talking about the work you concepted. Ideas you helped bring to life. Are you seriously telling me you're going to forget something essential about them? A detail here or there, perhaps. But what you'll discover is that these little details don't matter. (If they did, then by definition they'll be on a slide, so you can't forget them.)

Trust yourself to know your work.

And that's the other problem with notes. They erode your trust in yourself. Because you could nail everything you wanted to say… and then you have to check your notes. Just to be sure. And in that moment, you're displaying uncertainty to your audience.

Having notes and not needing them means you'll still check them. Skipping the notes entirely means you'll use your slides and trust in yourself.

And your audience will trust you in turn.

STOP TRYING TO MEMORIZE

Noted

I had a client who wrote notes more detailed than most movie scripts. Full-on sentences. Indications where they should pause for laughter or breath. Time stamps.

We went back and forth over those notes. I felt like a parent trying to break their aging child of a pacifier habit, or get them to part with a security blanket.

But the very first time I got them to present without notes, it was over. The sense of freedom they felt was totally addictive. In fact, they became so committed to just memorizing bullets and tossing notes that they insisted on the teleprompter being turned off during their talk.

They texted me afterward that a couple of folks from the c-suite told them they should speak for a living.

STOP EXPLAINING IDEAS

I'll say it again: your pitch is just another type of ad.

We know that emotion moves consumers more than logic. We say the same to clients every day. It's why we argue with our clients when they want us to promote a list of product features, as opposed to a single amazing benefit.

But when it comes to advertising our ads, we forget all of that.

We talk about features:
"This pre-roll will be unskippable for 5 seconds."

We state the obvious:
"You'll notice we placed the headline in all caps to really stand out."

We try to prove how smart we are:
"We'll use an illudium Q-36 space modulator and introduce the world to web4."

These are either matter-of-fact observations or grossly opaque statements. You'd never let your clients talk like that to their customers.

So don't talk like that to your clients.

To put it another way, they only need to understand the work enough to feel something from it.

Something like:
· Excitement for what it will do for their business.
· Relief for how it will solve their problems.
· Pride in how it will make people view them.

When talking about the work, the goal isn't to be complete. It's to be compelling.

Which is why it's way less important that they understand everything about the work than you think. In fact, the more you try to expand their understanding, the more likely you are to kiss that idea goodbye.

START PUTTING WOW BEFORE HOW

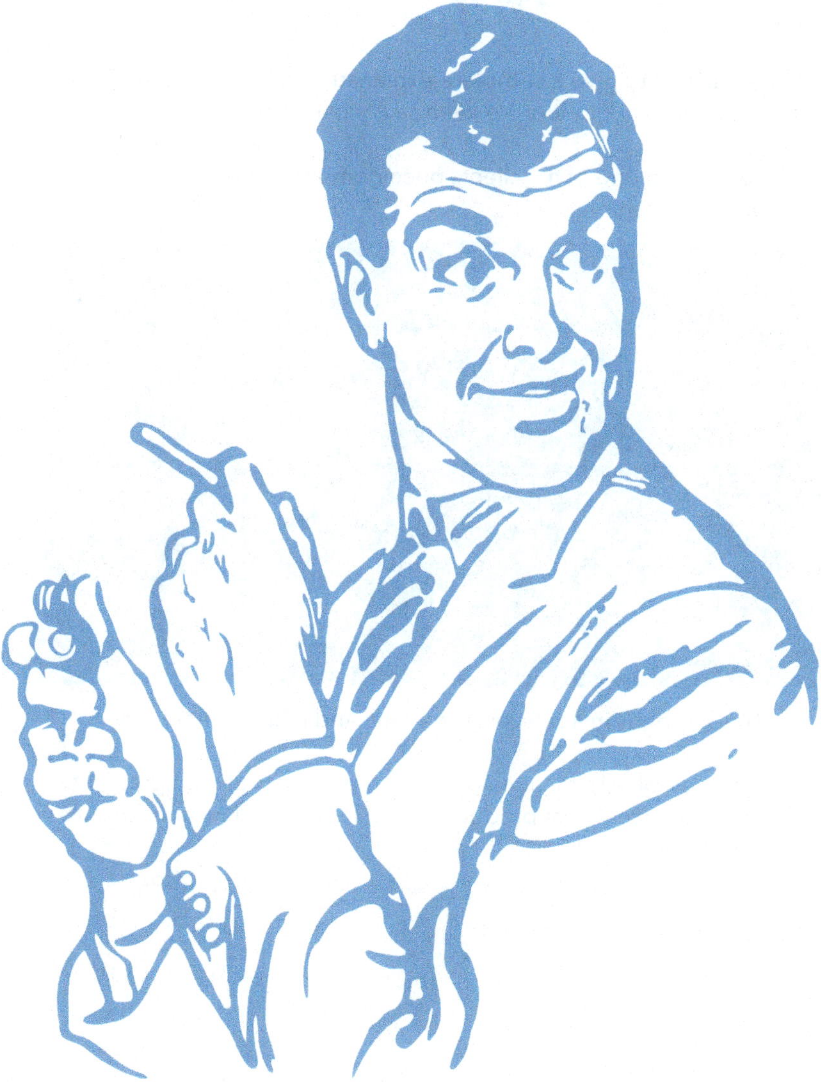

START PUTTING WOW BEFORE HOW

In our zeal to give a complete explanation, we often cover "how" our ideas work before we even say "what" they are.

Something one of my clients once demonstrated in dramatic fashion.

Direct Confusion

I worked with an ECD who did a brilliant job explaining *How the World Is* and *How it Could Be*. I (playing the client) was ready to hear their solution to my problem. Then they said, *"We're gonna get nine directors."*

Hunh? Like...film directors? Directors of traffic? Art directors?

"Each of these directors? They're going to bring their own unique take to our vision."

Ok, so...probably film? Or, like, a Director of Choreography?

"And then we'll allow each of them to make their own anthem spot."

Ah, we're talking about commercials. Ok. Phew.

This happens in agencies every day. And I think I know why.

Chronologically, the idea is one of the first things we figure out. Then we race it past production and legal and dev to make sure we can make it.

STOP EXPLAINING IDEAS

Which means we get to the meeting and dive into the thing we just spent all this time on: the production. We want the client to know that we've done our homework.

But it has the exact opposite effect.

It's like if I introduced myself by saying, *"Hi, I'm Ben and I'm super honest! You can trust me!"*

It might be true, but it's weird to bring up. Feels very untrustworthy, in fact.

The same thing happens in meetings. The harder you try to explain every single detail of an idea, the less convinced clients will become that it's gonna work.

It's also super annoying to listen to. Here, I'll show you:

Imagine you've just finished a great meal and ask the waiter what's for dessert.

"Well, the chef is in the kitchen with a bowl. He's mixing milk, eggs, and flour together in there. Meanwhile, the oven is heating to four hundred degrees. And there's fresh fruit he's sprinkling with powdered sugar…"

How frustrating is that answer? He's going on and on and you still have no idea what the dessert is. That's how your clients feel when you start with "How" before the "Wow."

"MAGNIFIQUE!"

If you're gonna bring the Wow, you need to do two things:

- Tell them what the idea is
- Tell them why it matters to them

It's probably going to feel too simple. But simple is good. Simple is the first step before you get to complex. Walking before running, and all that.

What...
"We're going to retell classic Fairy Tales in three frames, using Boost Mobile technology."

"We're going to give Heinz its own IMDB page and take credit for every single scene our bottle appeared in."

"We're going to let marathoners and their fans communicate mid-race."

...plus Why
"We're going to retell classic Fairy Tales in three frames, using Boost Mobile technology. Demonstrating the impact Crazy Fast speeds can have in your life."

"We're going to give Heinz its own IMDB page and take credit for every single scene our bottle appeared in. Instantly proving our legacy and becoming the biggest star on film or screen."

"We're going to let marathoners and their fans communicate mid-race. Proving that Liberty Mutual has you covered on the road- in your car, or in your sneakers."

STOP EXPLAINING IDEAS

START BEING GENERALLY RIGHT OVER PERFECTLY CORRECT

In fairness, you will have to explain some of the "how" behind your concepts. No client will approve work they don't understand. The caveat is that "understand" is a spectrum.

At one end, there's utter confusion. And at the other, there's mastery. However, neither extreme is conducive to selling your work. The goal is to ensure your audience quickly grasps what you're discussing without the need for immediate deep dives, complex details, and PHD-level asides.

Metaphors, analogies, and examples are your best friends.

I once heard someone say paying for college was like buying a brand new sports car and pushing it off a cliff.

Every year. For four years.

As soon as they said it, I had a whole new appreciation of what this was going to feel like financially for my family.

Except...

The more you think about that analogy, the less it works. College is an investment, you're not just tossing the money off a cliff. And how does that person know how much I spend on college anyway? Tuition at community colleges is way less than a sports car. This analogy is awful!

But hang on- it's only awful if your goal is to be perfectly correct. If your aim is to express to your audience that college will drain your financial resources on a scale they've never experienced before, it's a great starting point.

So stop trying to be a perfectionist when explaining your work. Get it generally correct, so that your audience gets the emotions you want them to feel.

Some of us (myself included) absolutely love the part of this job that comes from figuring out how to make our ideas real. And because we love it, we really wanna talk about it. Especially if it falls into the categories of "new" or "innovative".

But our clients do not care. And I'll prove it. Using a microwave.

I use a microwave daily. I haven't the faintest idea how it functions. Despite every frozen food package imploring that I adjust my cooking time accordingly, I'm not even sure what "power level" it is.

But I would never question the need for a microwave in my kitchen because I understand what it does.

And that's where all the agencies pitching innovative, bleeding edge, non-fungible tokens/Blockchain/Web3/Meta/AI concepts keep shooting themselves in the foot.

They go on and on about how it works. Not what it does.

And inevitably this is the part where someone says, "But my client wants to know all the details!"

So, let's go there.

STOP EXPLAINING IDEAS

START UNDERSTANDING WHAT YOUR CLIENT NEEDS TO KNOW

Yes, clients might ask how an idea works. But they don't actually care about the details. What they want to know is *"Have you got this?"* They want to know that the agency isn't completely full of bovine excrement and what you're promising is doable.

This may mean you have to give your clients a general overview. It doesn't mean you need to give them a doctorate in the production details.

They're just feeling unsure of this new thing. They're asking questions so you can make them feel confident that you've thought things through, so they don't have to.

Just hit the high notes. Like my microwave timer.

START USING ANALOGIES AND METAPHORS

The best ideas are often unique, complex, or risky. Which means clients are unlikely to choose them unless they become comfortable with these factors.

Analogies are a triple threat here.

- They anchor your idea in a cultural reference the client "gets"
- They link a known behavior to your unknown concept
- They provide anecdotal proof that this has worked in the past

Example time! Here's how I explain the collectible NFT trend to people without mentioning blockchains.

(No one may remember what the collectible NFT craze was about by the time this book is published. Think beanie babies, but JPEGs.)

It was a confusing time for clients. They wanted to jump on this massive trend but couldn't understand it.

Why the hell was anyone paying money for a picture of a cartoon monkey that anyone else could download for free?

NFTs are complicated as hell. I could start by talking about blockchain technology. Or perhaps decentralized computing and the rise of cryptocurrency. Or maybe about how this was all co-opted by the fine art market...

Does your head hurt yet? Mine too. And the deck would have to be forty-five slides long before we get to the work. Which is why I don't explain any of that.

Instead, I talk about baseball cards.

"You can find a picture of any baseball card ever printed online. However, only the original card sells for hundreds at auction.

The picture is the same. There's no extra information on the card, but because people value the original, they pay more for it.

The collectible NFT craze is like baseball cards. It's not about the image; it's about what it means to have the 'actual' version of the graphic. Even though it's virtual."

After hearing the above, your client still won't understand NFTs. But they understand collectible crazes. So, they can approve it without a doctoral thesis in crypto.

In fact, if you want to get technical about how I didn't get technical, I didn't explain how NFTs worked. I explained the *behavior* around them.

Clients don't need to know how something works to buy it. What they need to know is why it works.

84

The best analogies will have:
- A cultural reference your audience understands (obscurity is the enemy)
- A similar functionality (baseball cards aren't much different from their pictures)
- A benefit that matches your idea (collectors spend thousands on cards)

The right analogy will have the client understanding why to buy your idea, even if they don't understand how it works.

START BEING SELECTIVE WITH YOUR ANALOGIES

When you're going to use an analogy, make damn sure the analogy carries the same meaning for your audience as it does for you. Here's what I mean.

I once had a client who was pitching for a car account. They wanted to talk about how their proprietary process was a new evolution in advertising. Like what the assembly line meant for Ford.

I politely discouraged this idea.

Here's why. To someone outside the car industry, an association with assembly lines is probably going to be surface level. It's just about evolution.

But to an automotive insider, the phrase "assembly line" is going to be drenched in different associations: timelines, budgets, and union disputes. They're not going to feel the same thing you are because they're too close to it.

In fact, I generally try to pick analogies that come from outside the audience's professional life, to avoid the risk of this happening.

STOP FABRICATING DRAMA

It's entirely possible that at this point you're saying, *"Ben, when you talked about How The World Is, you referred to it as twisting a knife in the client! You're nothing but drama!"*

To which I would hypothetically say, *"You're right, I'm all for drama. But it needs to be honest drama. Not the cheap surprise that most creatives seem contractually obligated to cram into their decks."*

Over and over again I've seen folks hold out on sharing critical information because they want to artificially delay the moment it all comes together. They think the longer they can put things off, the greater the reveal will be when it finally comes.

But delay of gratification does not automatically equal drama. There's a difference between surprise and suspense.

START USING SUSPENSE OVER SURPRISE

Writing a book is an exhausting undertaking.

So I'm going to take a break and let Alfred Hitchcock explain this:

"We are now having a very innocent little chat. Let's suppose that there is a bomb underneath this table between us. Nothing happens, and then all of a sudden, 'Boom!' There is an explosion. The public is surprised, but prior to this surprise, it has seen an absolutely ordinary scene, of no special consequence.

"Now, let us take a suspense situation. The bomb is underneath the table and the public knows it, probably because they have seen the anarchist place it there. The public is aware the bomb is going to explode at one o'clock and there is a clock in the decor. The public can see that it is a quarter to one. In these conditions, the same innocuous conversation becomes fascinating because the public is participating in the scene. The audience is longing to warn the characters on the screen: 'You shouldn't be talking about such trivial matters. There is a bomb beneath you and it is about to explode!'

"In the first case we have given the public fifteen seconds of surprise at the moment of the explosion. In the second we have provided them with fifteen minutes of suspense."*

Thanks, Alfie. You can go back to your eternal rest now.

*Truffaut, François. Hitchcock. Simon & Schuster, 1985.

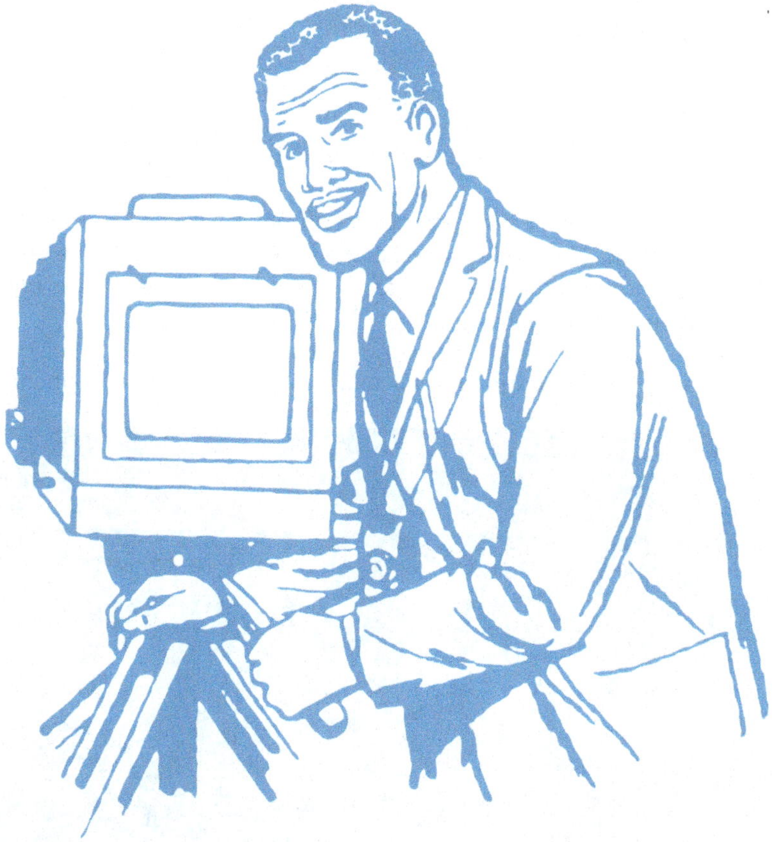

The truth is that agencies are addicted to revealing moments. We're constantly trying to make the transition to the next concept slide into a big deal.

But unless we've put time into telling the story correctly, we resort to cheap surprise moments. We hold back relevant information until the last second. That doesn't build suspense. It builds resentment.

If we communicate the concepts properly, we won't need to hide anything. The suspense will come from understanding the ending we propose (their success) and wondering how we're possibly going to make it a reality.

If it's good enough for Hitchcock, it's good enough for our concepts.

Suspense, by any other name

"Romeo and Juliet tell you the titular characters are going to kill themselves in the second sentence."

I was running a group training when one of the participants told me this. I couldn't believe it. But it's true.

The Bard ruins the surprise a sentence and a half in. And yet it's one of the most enduring storylines of all time.

So don't be afraid to tell your audience what the solution is. Let the suspense come from wondering how you're going to make it happen.

After all, I've seen the R+J story 100 times. But if Michael Bay does a remake, I'm buying a ticket.

I have GOT to see how that happens.

STOP CREATING DRAMA

START AVOIDING WORDS LIKE EPIC, AWESOME, AND AMAZING

Sometimes, when we try to bring the Wow, we make the mistake of telling our audience how we want them to feel.

"We have this amazing idea…"
"We're going to do this in a really epic way…"
"This is really awesome…"

When you tell someone how they should feel, the response is for them to metaphorically (sometimes literally) fold their arms, lean back in their chair, and go, *"Oh, really? I'll be the judge of that."*

It turns your excitement to poison. They want to prove you wrong. So, show them how it's amazing. Set them up with the benefit. Just don't tell them how they should feel.

"What's the deal with intros?"

Jerry Seinfeld once reamed out his opening act for introducing him by saying, *"And here's the best comedian in the world- Jerry Seinfeld!"*

Jerry went out, did his whole act, walked off stage, and immediately went over to the opener. *'You never put that kind of pressure on a comedian! You say that and everyone goes 'Oh, really…'.'*

Don't piss off Jerry Seinfeld. Or your audience. Don't tell them how to feel.

STOP USING INFO-GRAPHICS

7

START
UNDERSTANDING THE FUNCTION OF GRAPHS

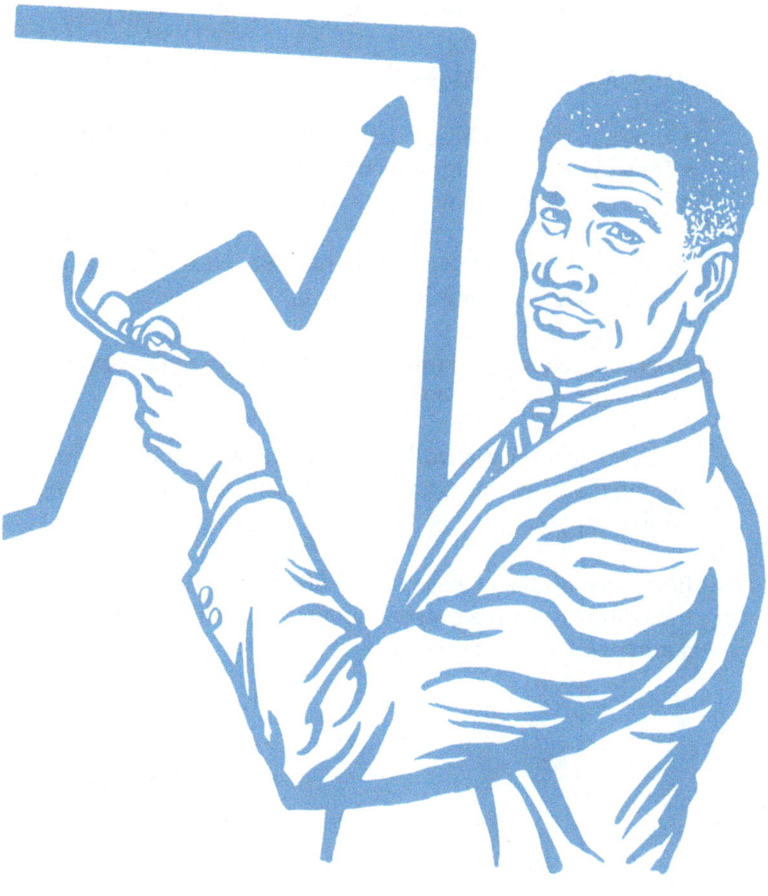

START UNDERSTANDING THE FUNCTION OF GRAPHS

Many people think that the perfect chart, graph, or infographic is the secret to simplifying their slides.

To be fair, graphs do have their uses.

- They can contextualize numbers that otherwise look drab
- They can distill paragraphs down to a single representative chart
- They can clearly demonstrate relationships and trends

They can also get thrown in the trash. Because they're almost never the best way to do any of the above.

The trouble with graphs, charts, and the like is that they're the concluding paragraph of a five-page research paper.

If you've done all the work to fully understand those things ahead of time then yes, this is a wonderful distillation of *everything*. Well done, you.

But if your audience hasn't done any of that (and if they have, why in the world are you re-presenting it to them?) then this isn't a brilliant summary, it's math homework.

STOP USING INFOGRAPHICS

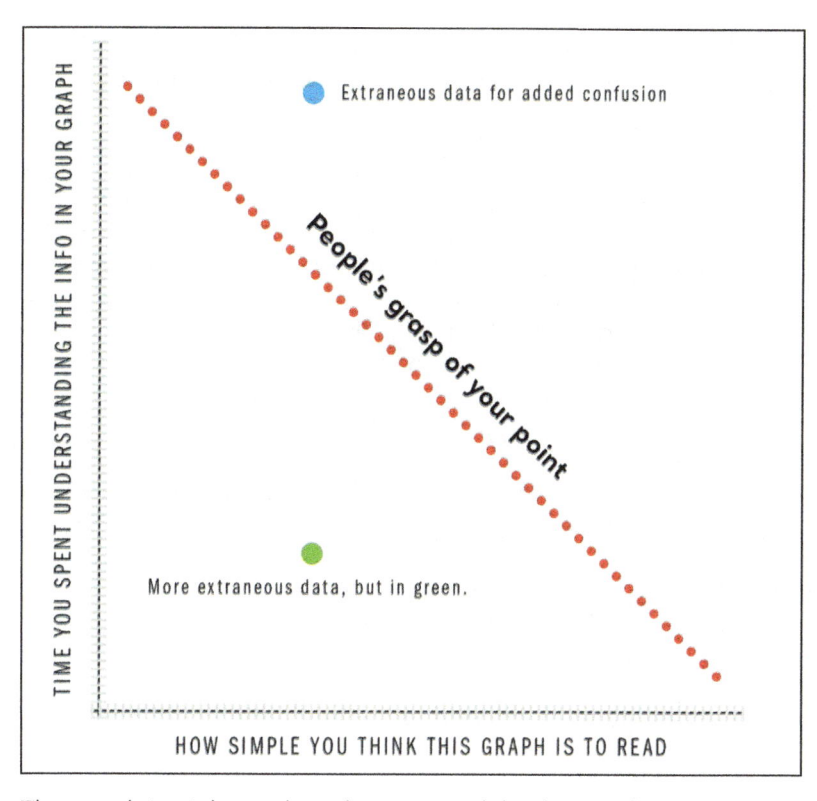

[Graph with y-axis labeled "TIME YOU SPENT UNDERSTANDING THE INFO IN YOUR GRAPH" and x-axis labeled "HOW SIMPLE YOU THINK THIS GRAPH IS TO READ". A descending dotted line labeled "People's grasp of your point". A blue dot labeled "Extraneous data for added confusion" and a green dot labeled "More extraneous data, but in green."]

That graph is a joke, and you have as much background information as I do. All told, it's simple. But it still takes a second to "get it."

How much harder would it be if you had to understand "rising housing rates" and their relationship to "customer QR code download acquisitions since 2017"? Maybe color-coding a few trend lines would help? No? Of course not.

And that's the trouble with graphs. They don't really explain. They summarize.

You must back up and re-explain all the various axes, how they relate, and what someone is supposed to take from it all.

If you want to use a graph correctly, you must use it as the concluding point of your argument. You have to set it up by explaining the X-axis on a slide. Then, the Y-axis. Then, all the various contexts and work required so that when you finally land on the chart, the audience goes, *"Aah, we get it now."*

I did say graphs should "almost never" be in your presentation. So, when is it ok to chart it up?

When the output is emotional.

The goal of your pitch should always be to connect emotionally with your client. Don't tell them something. Make them feel it.

And the right graph can absolutely make people feel something. Like this half-remembered chart a classmate made for their resume:

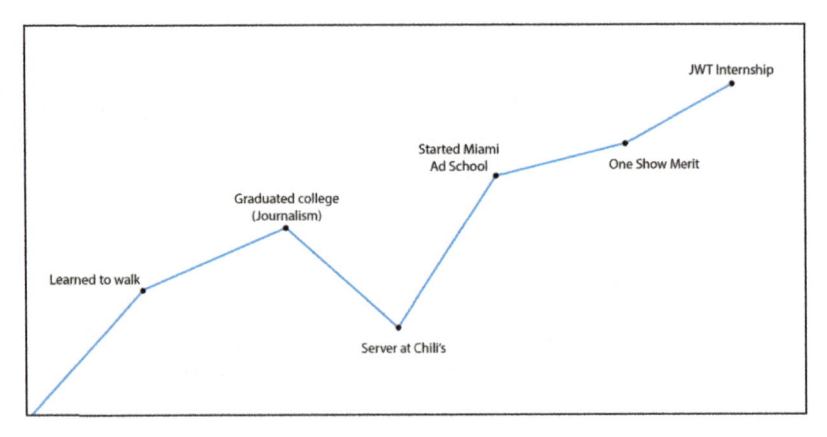

[Chart showing a life trajectory with points: Learned to walk, Graduated college (Journalism), Server at Chili's (dip down), Started Miami Ad School, One Show Merit, JWT Internship]

STOP USING INFOGRAPHICS

It's simple. Emotive. The graph makes us think about things in a whole new way. It does everything good data visualization is supposed to do.

It's practically a piece of advertising.

Here's the catch though: good infographics take time. For most of our pitches, time is what we do not have.

This is why most people simply toss their data points into Excel and create a pie chart. Which, shockingly, does not create an emotional connection beyond disappointment.

This is why I usually defer to a single image to emotionally connect my data to my audience.

STOP SOUNDING PROFESSIONAL

"People will forget what you say, but they will never forget how you made them feel."

Maya Angelou's original quote was a little longer, but that really just proves her point. We all feel the truth of this sentiment.

And science agrees.

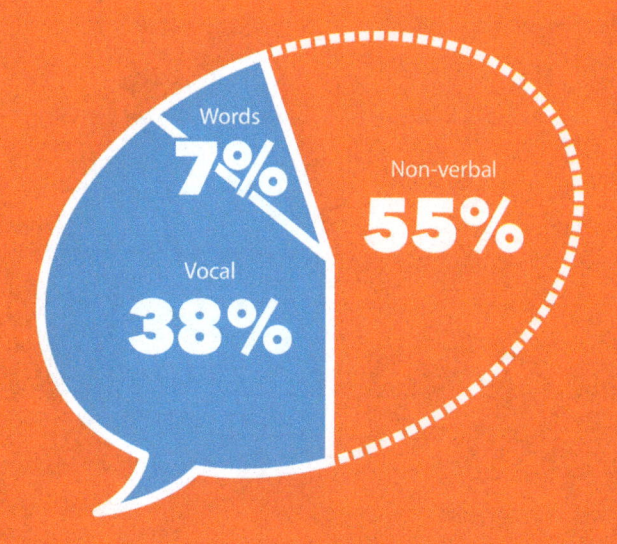

Words
7%

Non-verbal
55%

Vocal
38%

There's an oft-quoted study* claiming word choice represents just 7% percent of communication, while 38% comes from tone and expressiveness. There's some debate about the precise percentages, but you can't deny that how you speak is an integral part of delivering your message.

Want a fun example? Ask Alexa any question requiring more than a two-sentence answer. Like nails on a chalkboard, isn't it?

*My editor informed me that if I don't cite the study, I'll sound like a fraud. So here you go: Mehrabian, Albert (1971). Silent Messages (1st ed.). Belmont, CA: Wadsworth. ISBN 0-534-00910-7.

START LEVERAGING PITCH, PROJECTION, AND PACING

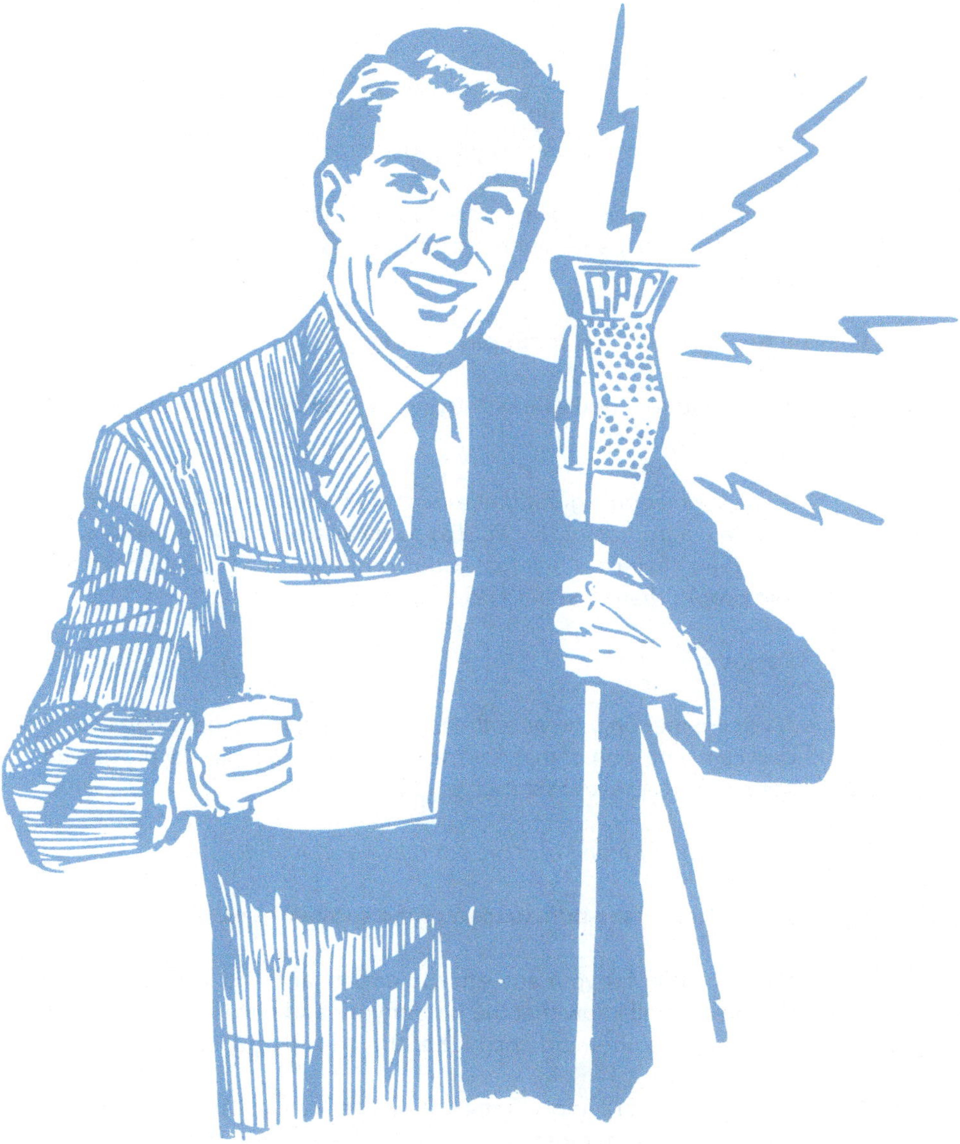
CPC

There's another reason why your tone is so important.

Neuroscience has shown that the more uniform the delivery of information is, the harder our brains have to work to absorb and parse it.

In plain English: boring stuff is harder to pay attention to.

It's the auditory equivalent of trying to absorb the Gettysburg Address like this:

…We are met on a great battle-field of that war we have come to dedicate a portion of that field as a final resting place for those who here gave their lives that that nation might live it is altogether fitting and proper that we should do this…

Versus this:

…We are met on a great battle-field of that war. We have come to dedicate a portion of that field, as a final resting place for those who here gave their lives that that nation might live.

It is altogether fitting and proper that we should do this.

Put simply, verbal delivery is the punctuation of the spoken word.

Make it easier for your audience to understand and listen to you. Because we all know that the harder your audience has to work to understand something, the higher the odds they'll just tune it out.

This is even more important if your audience can't see you. Like if you're camera-off for some reason, or the meeting is taking place over a speaker phone in 1996.

If you want mastery over your voice, you need to understand the 3P's of speech: *Pitch, Projection,* and *Pacing*.

104

STOP SOUNDING PROFESSIONAL

START UNDERSTANDING PITCH
(THE TONE OF YOUR VOICE)

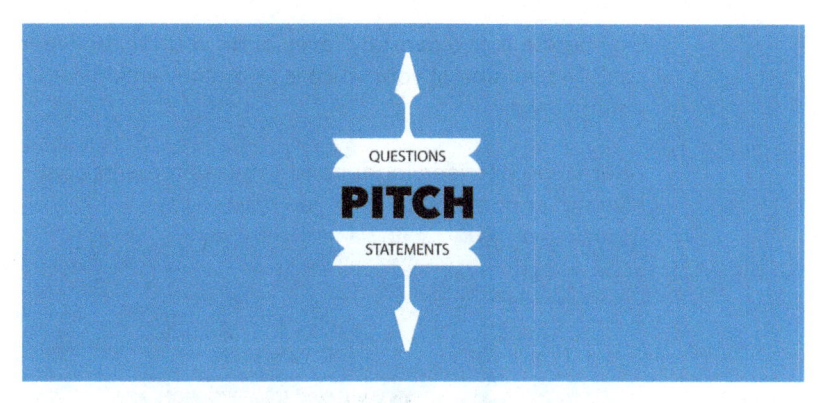

QUESTIONS
PITCH
STATEMENTS

Are you hitting the high notes? Do you ever go low? You don't need to be a shrill cartoon character or the movie-announcer guy, but you should be varying scales.

In most cases, raising your pitch indicates a question. Lowering your tone usually denotes a "period" creating the feel of a definite statement.

For example-

"Where are my keys" pitched up at the end is a question.

"Where are my keys" pitched down sounds like an interrogation.

START
UNDERSTANDING PROJECTION
(THE VOLUME OF YOUR WORDS)

Do you speak at a constant level, or do you vary between loud and soft? The volume of your voice is frequently an indicator of your energy level.

Alternating between louder and softer statements conveys varying levels of importance to what you have to say.

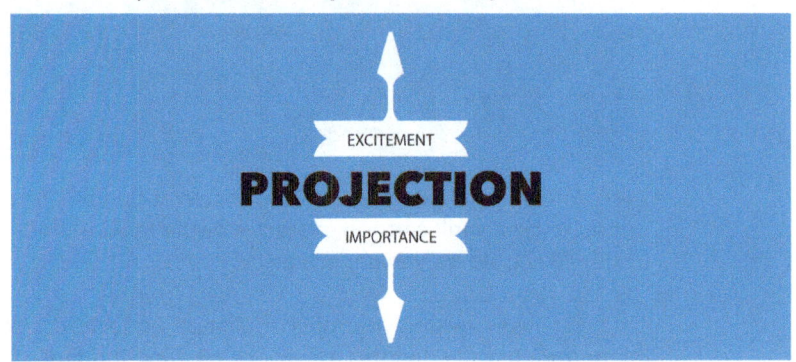

EXCITEMENT
PROJECTION
IMPORTANCE

In fact, speaking more softly is often the best way to get attention in a noisy room because it forces others to be silent to hear you. (Remember when your preschool teacher did this? You'd be shocked at how many teacher tactics work in meetings.)

So, make sure you're being judicious with your volume. Otherwise it turns into this:

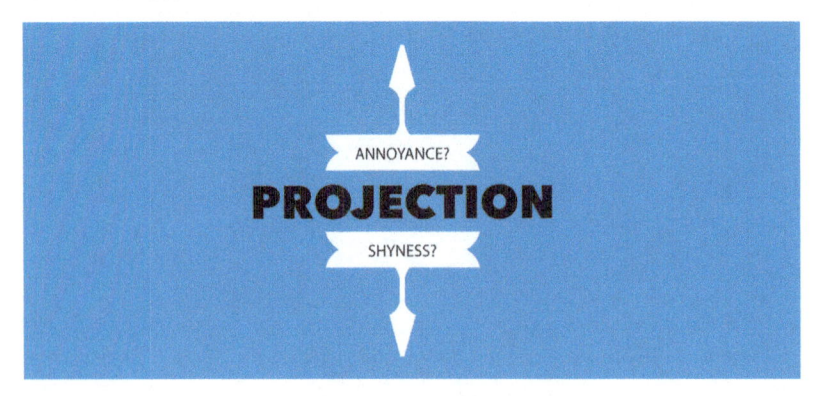

ANNOYANCE?
PROJECTION
SHYNESS?

STOP SOUNDING PROFESSIONAL

Louder for the client in the back

When I was first getting put in front of clients to present work, I had no idea what I was doing. In fact, I believed my job was to say and do as little as possible.

My CD at the time pulled me aside and said, *"You could be a little more excited about the work when you present."*

SO I TALKED LIKE THIS FOR THE NEXT SIX MONTHS.

It, uh, didn't work.

You can't just break the knob off at 11 and think that makes you excited. You need to create the appropriate emphasis by varying your projection.

START
UNDERSTANDING PACING
(THE SPEED OF YOUR DELIVERY)

⬅ SERIOUS **PACING** EXCITED ➡

Is your excitement reflected in your pace? Do you slow down to let big ideas sink in? At the very least, are you comfortably pausing for breath?

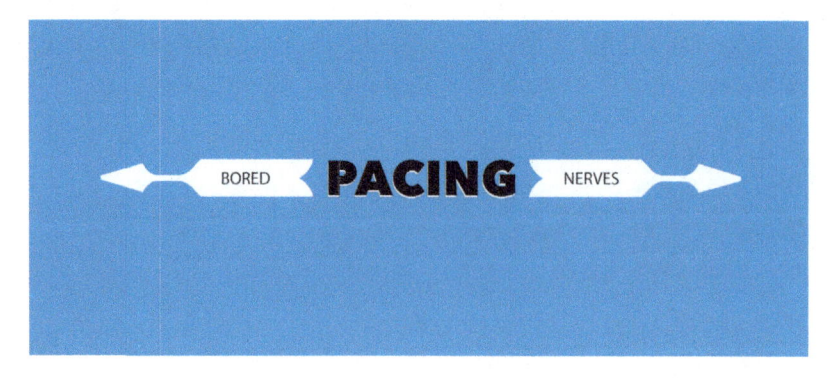

⬅ BORED **PACING** NERVES ➡

Speak too quickly for too long, and you can appear nervous or leave them behind. Speak too slowly for too long and you can put them to sleep.

Proper pacing turns a presentation into something like music, or a dance. It carries your audience along, racing with excitement one moment, pausing for reflection the next.

Pacing is also one of the biggest conveyors of confidence (more on that in a second). Once you control your pace, and use it consciously, you have reached a new level as a presenter.

PRACTICE EXERCISE: FINDING YOUR RANGE

What You'll Need:

· A children's book
· Your phone to record yourself

Authors writing for children employ a simple, easy-to-follow cadence. Their books have short phrases, meant to be emphasized at clear points. Unknowingly, we naturally leverage pitch, projection, and pacing when reading them.

I make all my clients do this. Yes, even the C-suite ones (especially them). Blackmail is a great tool for getting future freelance gigs. (I kid, I kid. Or do I?)

Listening to yourself read is a great opportunity to hear how you change pitch when speaking, what your natural range in volume is, and how pacing (even if it's just the space it takes to turn a page) can enhance the spoken word.

Now, compare the range of the three Ps you used here to your range when pitching. Are they different? How so?

Usually, people hold back in meetings because they're afraid to be themselves. If you think you sound warmer, more interesting, or more engaged when reading, consider how to bring those qualities into your pitch.

START USING THE SECRET 4TH P (PAUSE)

PAUSE
"..."

Technically speaking, a pause is just a further extension of pacing. But it deserves its own space when discussing speech.

The 'Pause' is the most powerful tool a presenter can use.

> When we pause, our audience's brains run back over the words we last said. This makes the pause the equivalent of bolding or underlining something in spoken language.
>
> In addition, a presenter who is comfortable using silence to speak for them will be perceived as confident.
>
> This is because silence feels "risky." By leaving space, you're allowing others to jump in, disagree with you, or even steal your spotlight. Displaying comfort with that risk is the ultimate presentation power move. That's why folks who never take a breath or cram their speech full of filler words convey nervousness.
>
> In the words of Miles Davis, *"It's not the notes you play; it's the notes you don't play."*

STOP SOUNDING PROFESSIONAL

START FIXING FILLER WORDS

Speaking of nerves, fewer things make folks more nervous than silence.

And because we can't handle the silence, we avoid it. Rushing through our pitches, asking rhetorical questions so we won't get interrupted, and never letting audiences get a word in edgewise.

And that, ladies and gentle-presenters, are where filler words come from.

Filler words are sounds you make unconsciously, unintentionally, or to cover a break in your speech. They're an insidious virus in your presentation. And just like a virus, you could have picked them up in a myriad of places.

START FIXING UMMM

Public enemy number one of the Filler Word Mafia. Ums can be short or long. They're often unconscious. And they're sneaky as hell. Most folks don't even realize when they say them.

Ums could appear because you're afraid of silence. So every tiny pause anywhere in your presentation gets filled by a sound. Um.

Ums can also come from nerves. They're the result of someone's mouth moving faster than their brain. They get halfway through a sentence, realize they're not sure what they're planning to say next, and insert a sound to hold the space while they figure it out. Ummmmmm.

If you suffer from the Ums, the first step is to train yourself to recognize them when they show up. This involves recording yourself speaking. This is horrible, I know. Sorry. Gotta be done.

Once you reach a point where you can sense the Ums as they're coming, work on replacing them with silence, or by taking a breath. And if your Ums come from speaking too quickly and running ahead of your brain, work on slowing your pace just a bit until your brain can catch up.

START FIXING LIKE/Y'KNOW/ KINDA/SORTA

These are like, the kinda words that, y'know, creep in when we sorta aren't sure how to like, describe stuff. Symptoms will usually just include one or two of these words. All four together are rare.

Folks usually catch this condition because they fell into the habit of speaking before they knew exactly what they wanted to say.

And so rather than making their point clearly and concisely, they drop in all these conditional syllables that make it hard to follow the plot. These words will soften their statements, steal their stage presence, and erode the power of their conviction.

The solution? Slower pacing and more breathing. And trusting that it's ok to say nothing for a second or two to gather your thoughts.

START FIXING RIGHT?/Y'KNOW?

These filler words habitually live at the end of a sentence, y'know? And the reason they're so bad is that they're not actually questions, right?

They're really shorthand for *"You know what I mean?"* and *"Do you agree with me?"*. And when they're deployed this way, at the end of every sentence, what they're saying is *"This is super scary for me right now and I need you to tell me I'm doing ok. Tell me I'm right. Or that you understand me. Just nod your head. Oh gawd, please give me a sign you don't hate me."*

In essence, these filler words are the presentational equivalent of you asking for a hug. Don't do it.

Unlike other filler words, pacing isn't the best way to tackle this. Once you become aware of them, focus on pitching your voice down at the end of a sentence. Speak with a sense of finality, so you can't reasonably ask a question simultaneously.

It can be hard to recognize filler words, even harder to rewire your habits to remove them. But here's a fun (for some people) exercise to help you do both. I give you: the "Um" Game.

PRACTICE EXERCISE:
THE "UM" GAME

What You'll Need:

- A friend (if you don't have one of these, just record yourself)
- A timer
- A list of random topics (There are sites you can use to generate this.)

The Rules:

- Have your friend pick a word out of the list.
- Tell them everything you can think of on that topic for ninety seconds.
- You cannot say "Um". Or "Uh" or any other filler sound which falls into that category. If you say "Y'know" a lot, then that's off the list too.
- If you utter any of the above, your turn ends immediately, and you choose a different word for your friend.

The first to speak for a full minute about a topic without dropping an "Um" wins! Feel great about yourself!

(If you're playing solo, go back and watch the recording to make sure you didn't say "Um" at some point without realizing it.)

There are two "tricks" to the "Um" Game.

The first is that you're allowed to take as long as you'd like between words. If you can control your pacing and become comfortable with silence, you will be able to win without a problem. If you're recording yourself, go back and see how you look when doing this.

Many people assume prolonged silence makes them look lost or confused. In fact, the exact opposite happens. They look thoughtful.

STOP SOUNDING PROFESSIONAL

The second trick is that if you take a moment and think about what you might say on a topic, you'll know where to go after you exhaust your initial thought.

For example, if I get "spaceship", I might start talking about astronauts. This is all good — until I run out of things to say about astronauts and then get stuck. But if I take a beat and associate a few different things — astronauts, living on the Moon, Mars — I've given myself somewhere to go after I run out of words on the first approach.

This applies when answering client questions, too. We're so quick to start speaking, we often start without knowing where we're going to end. Take a breath to think your answer through, and you'll rarely get lost.

STOP READING SLIDES

If there were a presentation 10 Commandments, Thou Shalt Not Reade Slides would be 1, 2, and probably 6. We all know not to read the slides.

Everyone tells us this.

Hell, I even have a sign up in my office that says it.

You know what's funny though?

Everyone tells you not to read slides. No one tells you what to do instead.

Which means we either
a) Read the slides anyway, or
b) Struggle to improv every synonym in the English language for what's on the slide.

A is obviously wrong, but hey, what's the real alternative?

B is a noble but doomed endeavor. After all, the slides were presumably put together by the best writers in the agency. People who literally write for a living.

Which means that not only are you attempting to freestyle synonyms under more pressure than a rapper spitting rhymes- you are attempting to do so without access to any of the best words.

You could make this harder on yourself, but you'd really have to work at it. Maybe present from a pool of flesh-eating Piranha with a slab of raw meat as a slide clicker?

The truth is, even if you're a lethal linguist who can lay bars straight off the dome, option B still won't work. Because...

Humans, on average, read two to three times faster than they speak.

Which means that by the time you're finished reading the slide to your audience, they've already read it. Twice.

You will quite literally be telling them something they already know.

9

START DOING THIS INSTEAD

STOP READING SLIDES

Here it is. You ready?

On the next page, I'm going to reveal to you
the answer to the most damning of all presentation mistakes…

STOP OVERWRITING SLIDES

No, you didn't miss a page. And this isn't a printing error. The truth is that the best way to stop reading slides is to stop overwriting them.

10

START THINKING OF VISUAL AIDES, NOT SLIDES

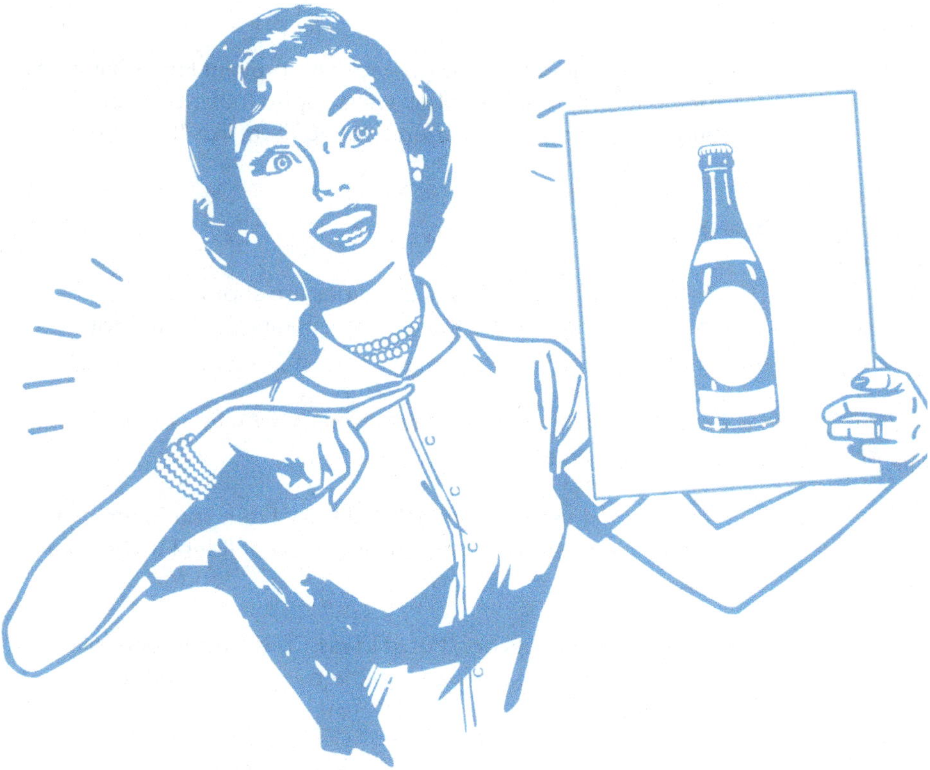

START THINKING OF VISUAL AIDES, NOT SLIDES

If I had a time machine, the first thing I would do is go back and kill baby Hitler. Obviously.

But the second thing I'd do is go back and prevent PowerPoint from ever being made. That was when we stopped looking at visuals in a meeting as "support" and started treating them like "the whole damn meeting."

And they're not.

They're visual aids. That means the slides are supposed to aid you in communicating the info that you are sharing. Aid you. Not replace you.

If all of the info is on the slides, then there's literally no reason for you to be there. The entire meeting should be an email.

A creative presentation is a transfer of trust. From you to the client. By the time it's done, you shouldn't just feel confident in the idea — they should too.

Here's the catch: clients don't trust ideas. They trust the people behind them. They are there to hire the people who will solve their problems.

Which means the focus of the meeting is you. Not the deck.

> "I just really trusted those slides."
> –No client, ever

STOP OVERWRITING SLIDES

START UNDERSTANDING HOW YOUR BRAIN PROCESSES INFO

The average concept slide looks like this:

ÜBEAR

Environmentally driven rideshare

It's the car on demand, without the carbon footprint. As consumers become increasingly eco-conscious, we have an opportunity to stand out from the crowd.

We'll get authentic wild animals (with limbs capable of controlling your average sedan) and put them in the driver's seat. We won't just be helping stranded happy hour guests, but the woodland community as well.

Along with being as environmentally friendly as humanly -or animalistically- possible, we'll be helping to finance environmental change.

This is problematic for several reasons.

First, because this slide is scientifically designed to mentally exhaust your audience. And I can prove it with a fun experiment.

Got a stopwatch? Get ready.

On the next page, there will be a series of circles. I want you to count them as quickly as possible.

Ready?

Go!

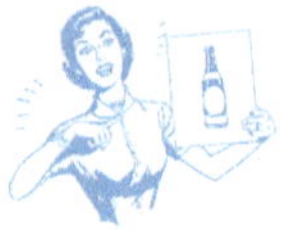

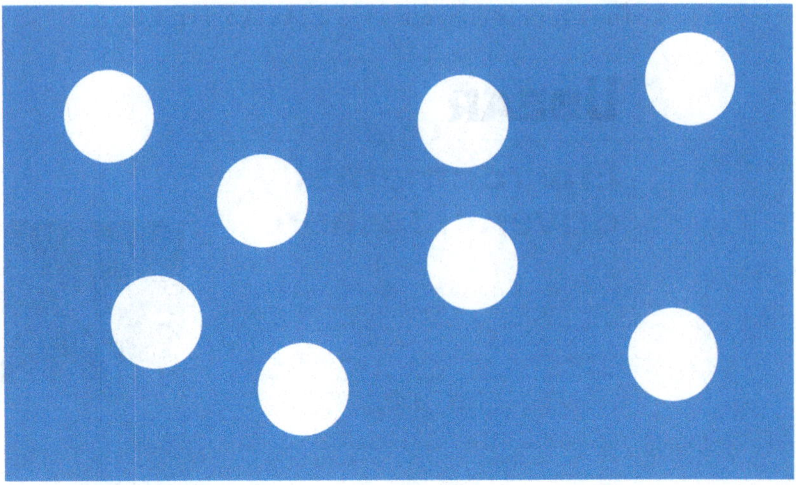

STOP OVERWRITING SLIDES

How fast were you? According to science, the average time it takes for someone to count all these circles is 0.8 seconds.

(You should have gotten eight. Every time I run this experiment in workshops, some hotshot shouts "SEVEN!" So, if you did, don't feel bad.)

Ok, one more time. Stopwatch ready?

Go!

128

I bet that was faster, wasn't it? According to science, about half a second faster (0.3 seconds to count them, on average).

It turns out that our brains don't see five or fewer objects as individual items. We quickly glance at it and just register the total sum.

But if you get over five items, we need to engage conscious effort. Very few of us can just "Rain Man" that first slide and instantly count eight dots.

Why does this matter? Because our brains are lazy AF.

I'd be offended by that, but it's too much work

"I'D BE OFFENDED, BUT IT'S TOO MUCH WORK."

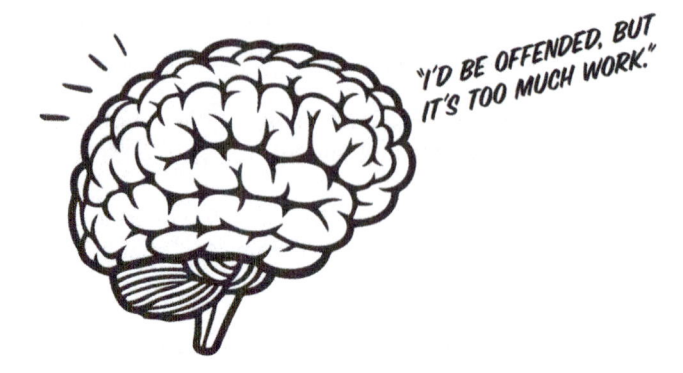

Human brains are constantly seeking the path of least resistance. This means that the harder you make your audience work, the more likely they are to tune out.

Let's look at that Übear slide again:

ÜBEAR

Environmentally driven rideshare

It's the car on demand, without the carbon footprint. As consumers become increasingly eco-conscious, we have an opportunity to stand out from the crowd.

We'll get authentic wild animals (with limbs capable of controlling your average sedan) and put them in the driver's seat. We won't just be helping stranded happy hour guests, but the woodland community as well.

Along with being as environmentally friendly as humanly -or animalistically- possible, we'll be helping to finance environmental change.

That is way more than five elements. Even if you want to count each paragraph as a single element – which isn't how this works – you're still over five. And don't forget to count the dividing line.

STOP OVERWRITING SLIDES

Speaking of those paragraphs, there's something else you should know about your brain – it's addicted to new information.

We get a dopamine hit when we learn something. That's why social media is so addictive. That's also why that statistic about people reading two to three times faster than they speak is so important.

Because it means that your info-addicted brain will ALWAYS prioritize the words over the speaker.

When you put up a slide like that Übear one, you're upstaging yourself with your own slide. You become a very distant second in everyone's mind.

START DESIGNING SLIDES LIKE BILLBOARDS

An ideal slide will have as few words as possible, and aim for no more than 5 total elements.

Or, to put it another way:

TREAT YOUR SLIDES LIKE YOUR BILLBOARDS.

For those who have never learned the noble art of out-of-home (OOH) advertising, there are three requirements:

- 7 words or less*
- Focus on image or words (not both)
- Needs to make sense at 60mph

Ok, you might not manage it in seven words. But shooting for that will keep you well below seventy.

When I share this point in workshops, I do it with that billboard image as my slide. It doesn't steal my thunder. It doesn't say anything I was going to say. And I don't even read it to the audience (they can do that for themselves, and have already done so faster than I could have said the words).

I COULD have shared the same information with a slide that looked like this:

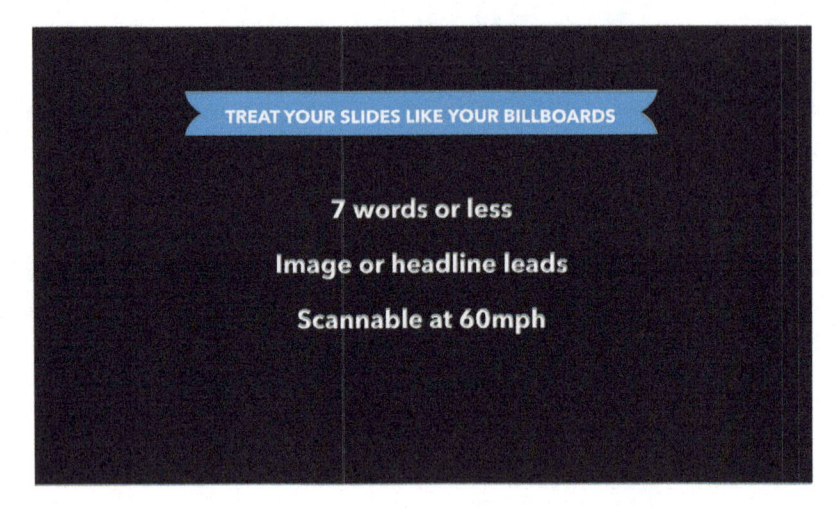

TREAT YOUR SLIDES LIKE YOUR BILLBOARDS

7 words or less

Image or headline leads

Scannable at 60mph

STOP OVERWRITING SLIDES

But that breaks our rule and leaves me with nothing to say.

So if you want to stop reading slides, stop making slides into Wikipedia-article-length diatribes about your ideas.

If I were to introduce Übear, that slide would go from this:

ÜBEAR

Environmentally driven rideshare

It's the car on demand, without the carbon footprint. As consumers become increasingly eco-conscious, we have an opportunity to stand out from the crowd.

We'll get authentic wild animals (with limbs capable of controlling your average sedan) and put them in the driver's seat. We won't just be helping stranded happy hour guests, but the woodland community as well.

Along with being as environmentally friendly as humanly -or animalistically- possible, we'll be helping to finance environmental change.

to this:

ÜBEAR

THE WORLD'S FIRST ENVIRONMENTALLY-DRIVEN RIDESHARE.

Or even this:

That first slide means this entire meeting could have been an email (all the info is in the deck). Meanwhile, the second and third are simply there to set me up to reveal the deeper story. I can present either of those without fear of reading slides, or being upstaged.

Yes, that bear is adorable. And he wears a hat better than I do. But he's still far less distracting to my presentation than a slide full of words.

START USING SLIDES AS NOTES

If you're struggling to decide what should go into the presentation and what should stay unsaid, here's your first clue.

If it's something you're worried about forgetting in the meeting, put it on a slide.

This doesn't mean the deck should be a script shown one slide at a time. It just means that anything you can't afford to forget should probably be shared with the whole class.

A statistic. A quote. The name of the client you're presenting to. If you're worried you're going to forget it, find a way to make it into a slide.

START USING MORE SLIDES

The billboard rule means that you're going to have fairly minimal slides. Which is what you want. Because (again) the slides aren't there to explain everything. They're there to set you up.

Think of it like a talk show. The slides are the host, you're the guest. Everyone's there to see you.

This is usually about the time in my workshops when someone panics and starts asking how in the world they're supposed to remember everything if the slide has just one line or picture on it.

Totally fair question. And I have a simple answer for you. Each point gets its own slide. Slides that look like this:

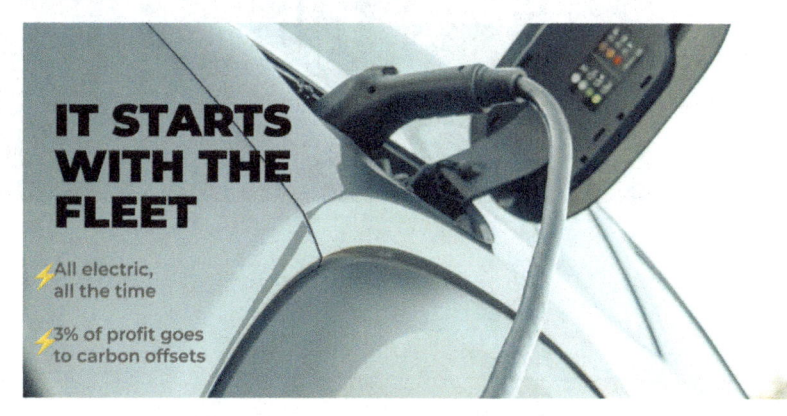

IT STARTS WITH THE FLEET

⚡ All electric, all the time

⚡ 3% of profit goes to carbon offsets

Or this:

ONE IS THE LONELIEST NUMBER

Synch calendars with friends

Get recommended travel times when the most people are headed the same way

Or this:

A LITTLE SOMETHING FOR MOM

Prompted to tip additional 1% to the planet.

STOP OVERWRITING SLIDES

Or this:

SPARE IT AND SHARE IT

Tiered badges to brag about all the good done commuting

These slides do break our billboard rule a bit. I allow myself a line or two, a bullet or two, to call out one detail.

You'll know you've gone too far if you have two separate points you want to express on a single slide. One point per slide is the rule. Any more than that, you're looking at multiple slides.

By doing it this way, I can ensure that my client is only reading and thinking about the point that we're discussing. Not reading ahead or getting distracted by too many elements.

In fact, there's a good chance you didn't take in those details about my brilliant Übear concept until just now, when you saw them all broken out.

START
UNDERSTANDING PRESENTATION VS DISCUSSION SLIDES

"My client wants to dig into the specifics! I can't do that with these slides!"

Then you can create a reference slide, like this:

SAVING THE EARTH SAFELY

Partnering with Raccoon Inc to protect identities

Double-blind calendar sharing means you can see names and times but not destinations or calendars

Token exchanges across proprietary network means safety from existing security flaws

Prompt always requires riders to opt-in, no automatic option

I want to be crystal clear– this is NOT a slide for presenting an idea.

You cannot control where your audience looks on this slide.
You cannot keep their attention focused on you. You cannot possibly finish talking about these ideas before your audience has read them for themselves.

There's no Wow here. It's all How. And that's ok, because the Wow already happened. It was in the slide before this.

A reference slide is the presentational equivalent of a map. It's there just to keep the conversation from going off-track. Nothing on a reference slide should be entirely new. It's a recap of the last several points you've made.

STOP OVERWRITING SLIDES

Some of you are looking at that slide and worrying that it still doesn't go deep enough.

If your audience needs to know more than that, it's not for you to explain in a creative presentation. Schedule a meeting between your experts and their experts, where they can happily speak expert-ese to one another while the rest of you look on in confusion.

It's not your job to get further in the weeds than this.

This does raise another question. If you're going to use this minimalistic/billboard approach throughout the entire deck, won't those decks get larger?

Yes. Yes they will.

So this seems like a great time to share with you the PERFECT number of slides in a deck. As proven by science, religious authorities, and AI chatbots.

That number is (drumroll please)...

"WHO GIVES A—"

START COUNTING YAWNS

No one cares how many slides are in your deck.

Just like a good ad, it's not the length that matters. It's how long it feels.

[I am so proud of myself for not making a dirty joke here. I think it shows I'm maturing as a person.]

Look, if you have 180 slides and you spend ten minutes on each, people will spend most of the meeting thinking of ways to murder you and hide the body.

But I've seen a single slide feel like 100, and 100 slides feel like half a dozen.

The number doesn't matter. It's about keeping it interesting. And a series of "billboard" slides are far more interesting than a "Wiki slide" any day of the week.

START USING THE ICEBERG DECK

"BUT I CAN'T SEND THESE SLIDES TO MY CLIENT!" I hear you cry.

Excellent! That's a great indicator that you have, in fact, created a perfect presentation deck.

Beary Funny

A friend of mine, who's spoken all around the world, understands this very well.

"I love when conferences ask for my slides in advance," he told me, *"It's like, 'Hey, slide 12 is just a full-bleed image of a koala eating eucalyptus. Have fun with that.'"*

STOP OVERWRITING SLIDES

Of course, this does present a problem. What the hell are you supposed to send to your client, who may forward it to folks who weren't in the meeting?

The solution is to build your presentation decks like icebergs.

Ninety percent of an iceberg's mass is below the surface (ask the Titanic). The same is true for your deck. Except by "below the surface" I mean "made invisible".

You start with a slide like this:

ÜBEAR

Environmentally driven rideshare

It's the car on demand, without the carbon footprint. As consumers become increasingly eco-conscious, we have an opportunity to stand out from the crowd.

We'll get authentic wild animals (with limbs capable of controlling your average sedan) and put them in the driver's seat. We won't just be helping stranded happy hour guests, but the woodland community as well.

Along with being as environmentally friendly as humanly -or animalistically- possible, we'll be helping to finance environmental change.

You start there because that is what you need to create to prove internally that you've fully thought through the idea.

But knowing what we know now, you make it a billboard slide:

So your deck will look something like this:

142

STOP OVERWRITING SLIDES

You've got those billboard slides, but also some info dump slides. Now hide the info dump slides.

Or minimize. Or skip. Or whatever command the software calls it. Every one of them has it. A function where the slides are still there but aren't visible.

Now, you can present without the info dump slides upstaging you.

When it's time to share the deck, just un-hide the info dump slides. Now you have a self-presenting deck with poster/headline intros before each full explanation. It's actually better paced than a deck that's just paragraph after paragraph, and didn't take you any extra work.

Having these info dump slides hidden during your presentation comes with another bonus. You can always reveal them in the meeting and use them the same way you would use the appendix.

Icebergs- great for deck structures, not so great for ocean liner structures.

STOP SABOTAGING YOUR CONCEPTS

Generally speaking, the literal ideas are the things creatives are most comfortable with presenting. But I wouldn't go so far as to say we're "good" at it.

We've covered slides, and Wow vs How. But there are still quite a few other creative presenter pitfalls to be wary of.

Choose to ignore these warnings, and you pitch at your own risk.

START AVOIDING CONCEPT JUICING

Hi. My name's Ben. And I used to artificially inflate my pitches.

I thought the smaller tactics in my campaigns weren't enough on their own. So I tried to make them sound bigger.

I over-hyped them.
Over-explained.
Over-sold.

I was concept juicing.

It never felt entirely right, but I was afraid to stop.
And I didn't know how to ask for help.

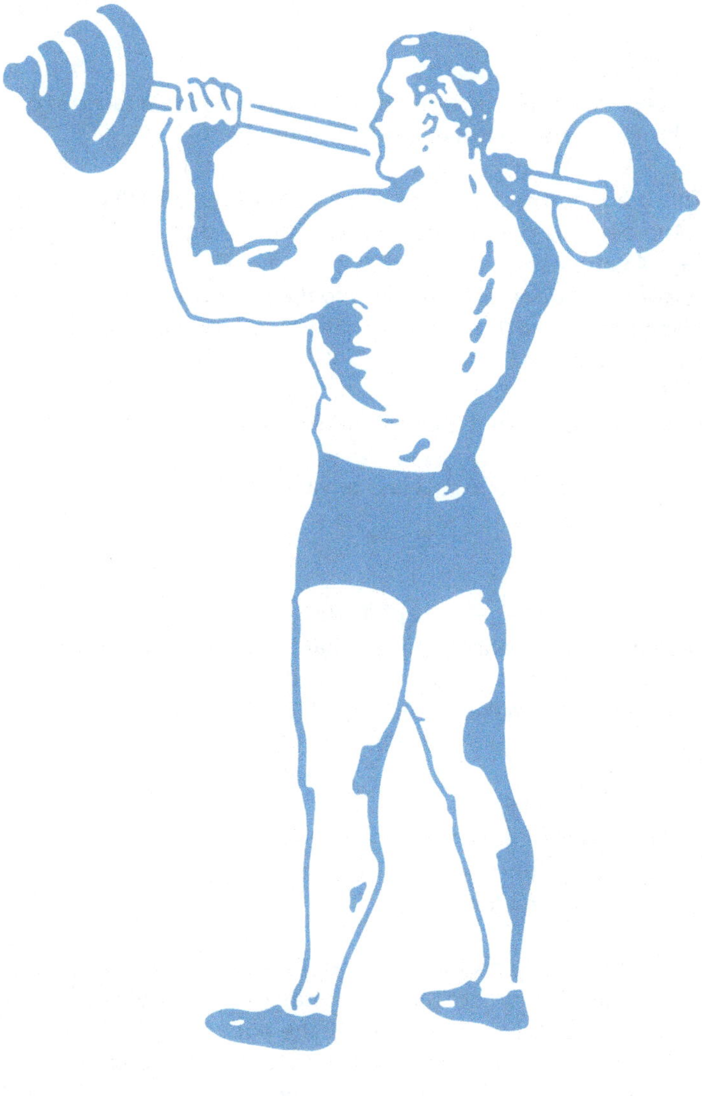

What is Concept Juicing?
Concept Juicing is the term for artificially inflating a tactic in order to make it seem bigger than it is. For example:

"This branded keychain is, as you can see, green. With your logo on it. And because people use their keys an average of 45 times a day, that's 45 impressions per person, per day. We've also sourced a supplier who does laser-etching, so the mark won't fade over time. Which means you'll continue to have that daily brand lift for decades to come."

Here's how to present the same idea, without the juice:

"As you can see, the logo works anywhere we put it. From a stadium roof to a keychain."

FAQs
Why do presenters Concept Juice?
Presenters often concept juice because they're afraid to spend "too little" time on a slide. So they desperately inflate the size of a simple tactic in a bid to make it seem equal to other ones.

What are the side effects of Concept Juicing?
— Loss of credibility
— Reduced client trust
— Approval dysfunction
— Looking like an idiot

What should I do if I suspect a coworker is Concept Juicing?
First, be understanding. Most of us have juiced a concept or two in our careers. But do not let them off the hook. Point out that they could not possibly be as excited about a 300x250 banner as they are about a Times Square takeover, nor should they pretend to be. If all else fails, show them these pages.

148

What if my coworker is doing more than just Concept Juicing?
Presenters who Concept Juice may also use Filler Words, Overindulge in Animation Effects, or suffer from Compulsive Over-explanation. If you feel they are in need of more help than you can provide, consult a professional like the one who wrote this book.

How I stopped juicing
Eventually, with the love of my art directors and caring CDs, I learned to present without juicing my concepts.

The key to presenting smaller tactics is to remember why they exist in the first place.

Of course a branded keychain, some banner ads, and a direct mail coupon aren't going to be as cool as an outdoor event or a cinema-quality video concept.

But they're not supposed to be. Their purpose is to continue to carry the bigger ideas forward. To keep the momentum going.

That's why I present smaller tactics as reinforcements of the big idea.

In a presentation, my talk track goes something like this:

"[Go big on the hype-worthy concepts. Introduce the campaign line. The key messaging. The art. Everything they're about to see all over again in 14 different formats...]

But we don't want this to be a single moment in time. So we'll make sure to remind our audience here–

[Flips to banner ads just long enough for clients to recognize the same message/art they've seen]

-and here-

[Flips to direct mail piece with the same vibes]

-and anywhere they're willing to spread our message.

[Flips to branded swag]"

When I present this way I'm not demeaning the tactics, but I'm not juicing them either. I just share them in a way that highlights their reason for existing – to support and enhance the larger idea.

If you or someone you know is Concept Juicing, sharing this information could be the first step towards a more effective and authentic presentation style.

STOP SABOTAGING YOUR CONCEPTS

START SAVING STORYBOARDS FOR DIRECTORS

Agencies usually present video concepts in one of two ways. And both of them are awful.

Awful option A: the script slide.

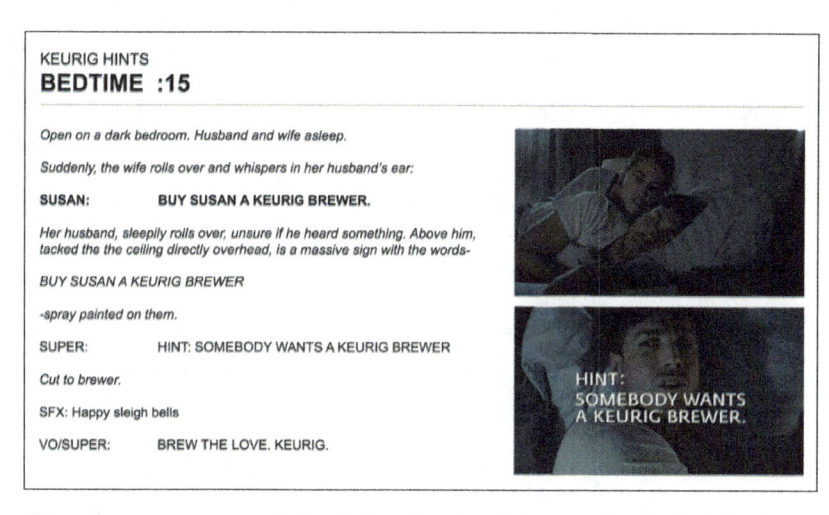

KEURIG HINTS
BEDTIME :15

Open on a dark bedroom. Husband and wife asleep.

Suddenly, the wife rolls over and whispers in her husband's ear:

SUSAN: BUY SUSAN A KEURIG BREWER.

Her husband, sleepily rolls over, unsure if he heard something. Above him, tacked the the ceiling directly overhead, is a massive sign with the words-

BUY SUSAN A KEURIG BREWER

-spray painted on them.

SUPER: HINT: SOMEBODY WANTS A KEURIG BREWER

Cut to brewer.

SFX: Happy sleigh bells

VO/SUPER: BREW THE LOVE. KEURIG.

There's too many words for this to be the right answer. So let's look at option B: the storyboard.

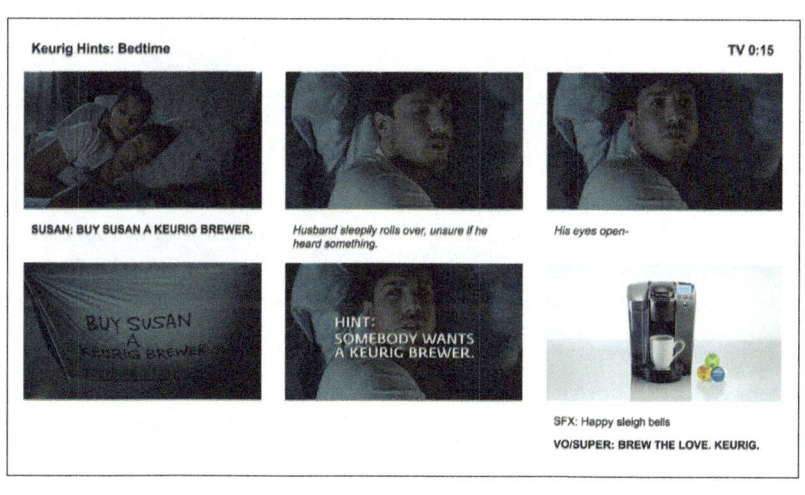

Well, that's more than five elements on a slide. On that criteria alone, both options are disqualified. Which isn't surprising- they're the wrong tools for the job.

Scripts and storyboards are fantastic tools… for producing your video concepts. They're ideal for helping talent and directors understand your vision.

But they're awful for helping clients to comprehend it.

The same reason you shouldn't lead with a script or a storyboard is the same reason that a builder doesn't lead with a set of blueprints. It's information overload. You lose the forest for the trees.

Instead, builders come in with a beautiful model or an incredibly detailed rendering. Something you can get emotional about.

This is why I don't want you to use your script or your storyboard to sell to your client.

There's just too much detail. Scene direction, special effects, camera motion – it's overwhelming. We think we need all that to get the client to appreciate our vision, but it's the opposite.

152

STOP SABOTAGING YOUR CONCEPTS

They can't understand it, and the excess detail completely wrecks any emotional impact or coherence.

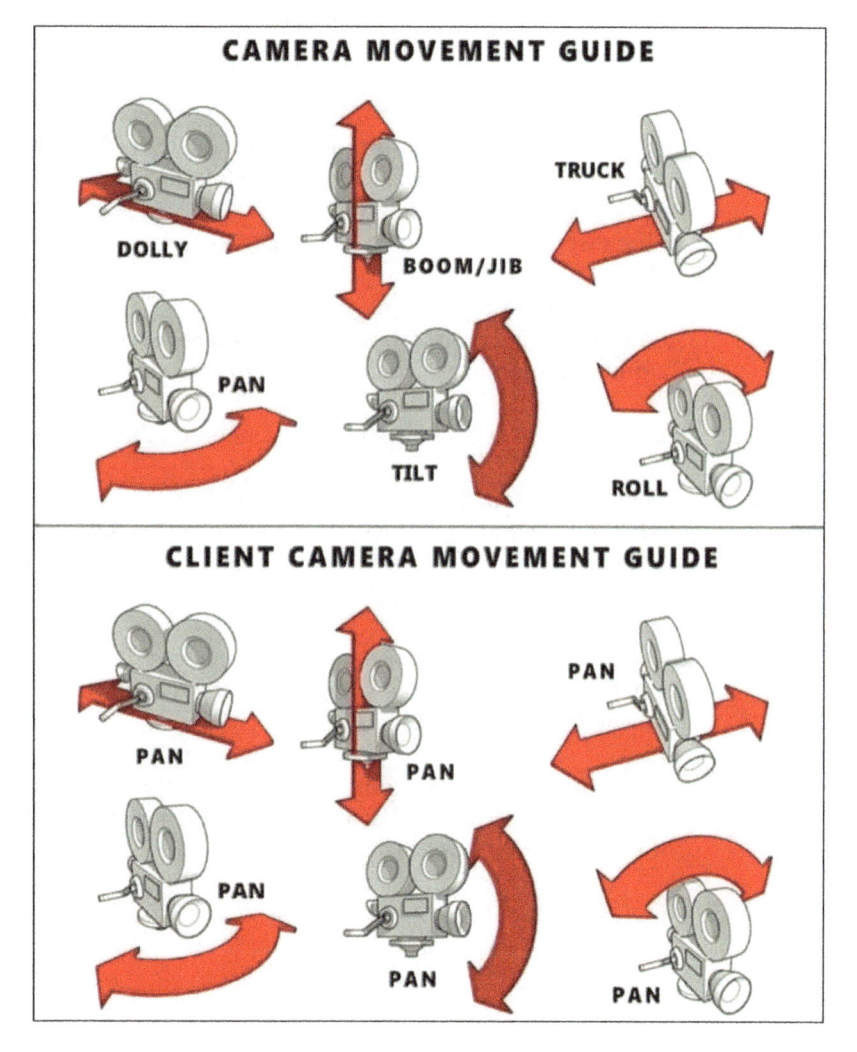

CAMERA MOVEMENT GUIDE

DOLLY — BOOM/JIB — TRUCK
PAN — TILT — ROLL

CLIENT CAMERA MOVEMENT GUIDE

PAN — PAN — PAN
PAN — PAN — PAN

Which is why, starting now, you'll present video like something intended to sell moving pictures: movie trailers.

START
IN A WORLD WHERE VIDEO PRESENTATIONS ARE ENGAGING...

Last time you asked a friend to see a new movie, did you start reading the script? Maybe printed out six 1x2 inch thumbnail images of the trailer for them to check out?

I'm guessing not.

You narrated the key parts that you found exciting, hoping to hook them with that and then fill in the details later.

That's what we should do with our clients.

The following is rated for all audiences
Start by getting rid of the words. Choose a key image for each significant moment or scene change in your script.

Each of those will be displayed full screen on their own slide.

Then you'll read the script to the client. Only the key points, and only what they need to get the idea. No bits of stage direction or a sound effect that doesn't matter for the main concept. While you do that, you will be paging through the visuals.

Think of it as a live performance of an animatic. Do this right and you'll give them a similar feeling to what they'd have watching the finished product.

Why? Because you are controlling their pacing. They only hear what you say, they only see what you show them, and there is nothing else for them to get distracted by.

It's just a beautiful shot of the forest. No worry about the trees.

Coming to a meeting near you
There are two-and-a-half important notes to this.

First, immediately after you perform the animatic, show them the script slide. You do this because they'll never be able to remember everything you said. And it's perfectly legal because the script is a specific type of reference slide. Since you've already presented the video, they'll have enough of the gist to not get lost in the details.

The real estate listings often do end with the floor plan.

First-and-a-half: This will add more slides to your deck. It's ok to reassure your audience that you will rip through the 215 slide deck in record time. Otherwise their souls might leave their bodies from pure shock.

Second, I realize you don't always have the time to prepare a series of beautiful visuals. In those situations, I pick a single key image and read the script over that. If I have even less time, I read the script while the name of the video is displayed. I can even ask them to close their eyes and put up a black slide while I read it to them.

But, critically, I never introduce them to the video while the words are visible.

START AVOIDING MOOD BOARD BLINDNESS

Today, on a very special episode of *Stop Reading Slides*…we're going to talk about an issue affecting hundreds if not thousands of presentations a day.

It's called Mood Board Blindness. Or MBB.

Mood Board Blindness (MBB) is responsible for hours of miscommunication with clients. Here are some of the symptoms:

- They focus on composition when you want their opinion on colors
- They comment on casting when you try to express lighting
- They look at geometry when you want to talk texture

Any one of these examples can thoroughly derail your presentation and harm your credibility.

And it starts with a single mood board.

Mood boards, like storyboards, are wonderful pre-production tools.

Their original purpose was to help creatives and photographers figure out "kinda sorta" what they were aiming for. They had to be imperfect because the final image didn't exist yet.

But that was ok, because the two parties were both super creative folks that could actually understand what all the hand waving and "y'know, like that, but totally different" really meant.

Clients, however, do not have that finely honed ability. (Hell, some creatives don't have it.)

So when you pull up a mood board, it's about as precise as those song lyrics you so meaningfully wrote in your middle school journal.

In other words, nobody's getting it but you.

STOP SABOTAGING YOUR CONCEPTS

START BY SETTING THE STAGE

There are a few scenarios where a mood board is an unavoidable part of a presentation. So, to help prevent Mood Board Blindness, remember the following:

If you must use a mood board, you must set the rules.

>Before those squares ever show up, tell the client exactly what they should be looking for- color, shape, texture, casting, light, composition, whatever.

>The truth is, that still won't prevent your clients from focusing on the wrong parts of the mood board. But it will at least improve your odds.

>And prevent the spread of MBB.

STOP TALKING TO YOURSELF

We have a terrible habit of treating our presentations like TED talks or commencement speeches. We run through the whole thing beginning to end without any desire for input from the audience.

And it's killing our chances of selling the best work.

START LEADING CONVERSATIONS, NOT PRESENTATIONS

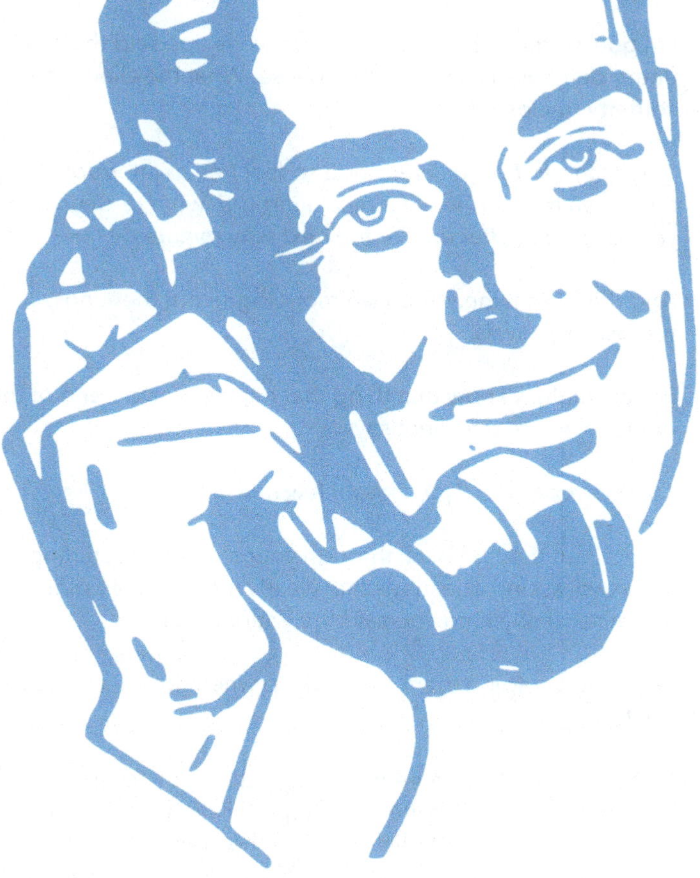

START LEADING CONVERSATIONS, NOT PRESENTATIONS

Raise your hand if you've ever told your client, *"I want this to be a conversation, so feel free to interrupt me at any time."* [Author's Note- The author's hand is up at this point]

Did it make your meeting any more conversational?

I'm guessing not. Probably because while you said the words, your entire demeanor said something else. What the client heard was something closer to:

"I want this to be a conversation so feel free to interrupt me at any time even though I won't indicate through word or deed that I want you to jump in after this for the next sixty minutes."

And that's a shame. When we monologue our meetings, we lose approvals.

For example, y'know that thing that happens at the end of the meeting where the client says:

"Thanks for all this, I just have a few questions…"

…and then they go back through your statements starting with slide two, asking questions that clearly indicate they didn't understand anything you said the entire time?

Yeah. Encouraging them to speak up when they're confused will fix that.

Or how about those meetings that end with the client just killing the work? No appeal, no hope for discussion. I imagine it's exactly how Roman gladiators felt in the arena.

Instead of waiting for the emperor to give a thumbs up or down to their opponent, you're watching the client do it to your idea, with even less chance to negotiate.

STOP TALKING TO YOURSELF

START EMBRACING ADDED BENEFITS

That binary decision-making gets nipped in the bud if you can get them talking early. More approval, less Aurelias.
Here's even more reasons to foster engagement in your meetings:

Keeps Things Casual
It's often been said that the agency meeting should be the most fun of the client's entire day. So don't monologue or be overly business-like. Create a dialogue, deepen the relationship, and maybe even make friends.

Indicates Interest
Clients feel like they're being included and treated as partners in a conversation.

Lessens Nerves
Engagement also offers you a chance to get some affirmation mid-meeting, since the audience responds to your points as you go. If you're nervous, getting a few nods or questions from the room that indicate they're paying attention and keeping up can do wonders for your blood pressure.

Speaking of which, engaging your audience with questions is a great way to take the pressure off. When they're answering, you're not talking. So, there's one less thing on your mind for a few seconds. Allowing you to literally and metaphorically catch your breath.

Creates Connection
Letting the client take part in the meeting increases the chance that they'll feel some ownership of the work as well. Feeling as though they're doing the work with you will make it that much harder for them to kill it.

And More!
Engagement also whitens teeth and puts 50 yards on your golf drive! Ok, I made those two up, but honestly, there's almost nothing engagement can't improve presentation-wise.

START ASKING BETTER QUESTIONS

It turns out there are stupid questions. At least if you want to create a dialogue.

The following are not good for starting conversations:

- "Does that make sense?"
- "Any questions?"
- "Following me so far?"

This is because they only allow the audience to display ignorance. No one has ever responded to one of these by raising a hand and saying:

"Actually, I'd just like to point out that I'm not as smart as my friends and colleagues in the room here. If you could just put the brakes on the entire meeting, just for me, and restart everything using smaller words, that would be great."

It's never happened. Instead, everyone thinks:

"Ok, I don't totally follow right now, but I'm a smart person. I bet if they keep going I'll be able to put things together and it will all click."

And then they give you the nod to keep going.

At best, you get a caveman-grunt of affirmation along with the nod.

A conversation, this is not.

Here's what I want you to ask instead.

Building Better Questions

What makes some questions better than others? The best questions do some or all of the following:

- Can't be answered 'Yes' or 'No'
- Highlight a pivotal moment in the pitch (reveal an insight, define a problem)
- Lead the client towards your next point
- Have answers based on opinions

Asking questions this way guarantees that your presentations will quickly become conversations. And I don't know about you, but I feel much more comfortable just talking to people than I do delivering a speech for their approval.

Can't be answered Yes/No

This is pretty obvious. I don't want you to ask them something that can be answered monosyllabically. The goal is to create conversation, not merely proof of life.

Yet, we often ask the question too deliberately, making the exchange useless. Take a look at these questions and see if you can improve on them.

PRACTICE EXERCISE: BEATING BAD QUESTIONS

What you'll need:

The following list of bad questions
- Who likes baseball?
- Do you ever make dinner for your family?
- How many of you think of palm trees when I say "Hawaii"?
- Who here drinks coffee?

What you'll do:

Rewrite the above in ways that avoid yes/no answers.

Then compare yours to the below. Note that those are not the only ways to rephrase the questions. I just want you to see how I tend to think about these things.

Do you have a sports memory that's meaningful to you? (Inclusive of folks who maybe just played sports as a kid, or watched with their parents, even if they're not active fans right now)

What's your favorite meal to cook for your family? (Even if all they do is make cereal, they can still participate in this answer)

When I say "Hawaii," what do you think of? (open ended)

What drink do you start your morning with? (Open ended and inclusive of the non-coffee drinkers)

Highlights a Pivotal Moment
When do you think the client is most engaged during a presentation? Asking this in workshops, I get all sorts of answers: during the creative, during the beginning, during the end when we solicit their reaction.

The real answer is much simpler: the client is most engaged when they're talking. Y'know, during literal participation. So those moments are most likely to be the ones they remember. Don't waste time focusing their attention and action on things that are merely transitional moments, or asides.

If I had to choose the best moment to ask a question in the entire presentation, it would be during the pivotal leap from info to insight.

If you do this right, your question will help them believe your research on an emotional level as well as an intellectual one. Let me give you an example.

Remember the *Boost Mobile Fairy Tales* pitch? If I had simply walked into the room and declared that no one knew what their tagline stood for, they might have gotten defensive. Instead, I asked them to define it for me, knowing that the answers would conflict. That way, their answers proved my point for me.

It's a lot harder to argue with yourself than the agency.

Leading the Witness
If we're going to talk about asking questions that lead to your next point, we have to talk about the number one fear folks have when I propose asking questions in meetings.

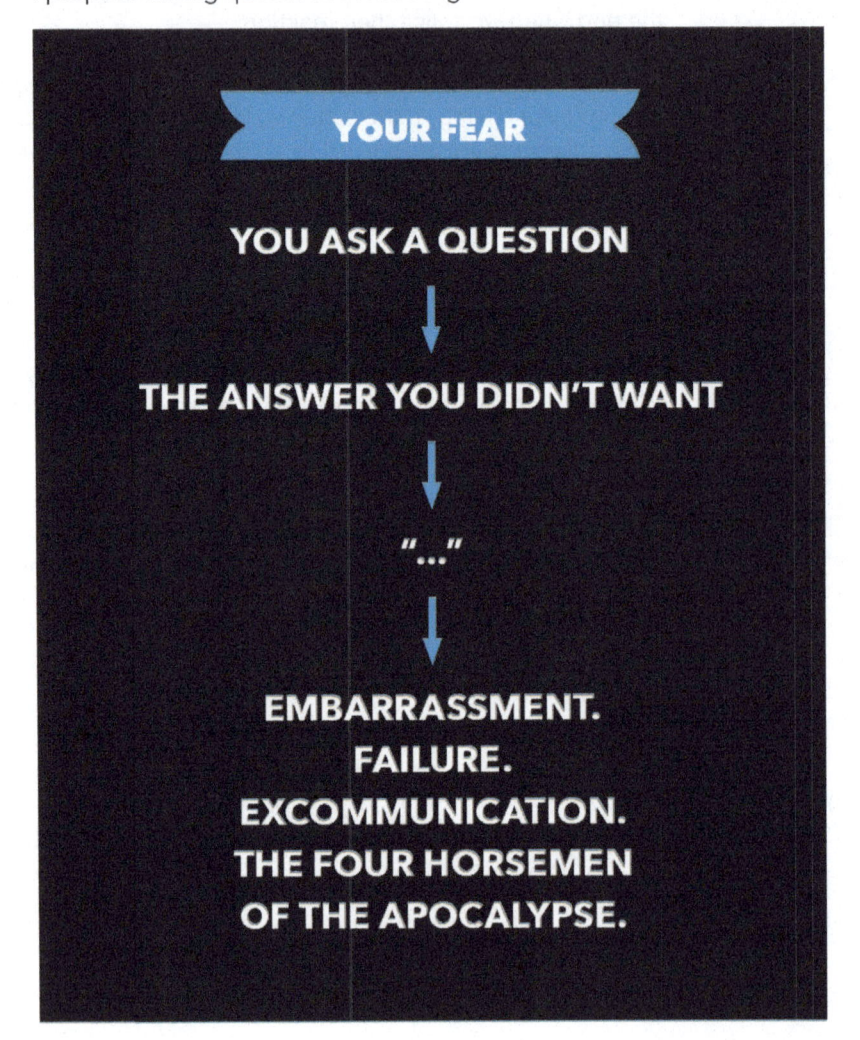

YOUR FEAR

YOU ASK A QUESTION
↓
THE ANSWER YOU DIDN'T WANT
↓
"..."
↓
**EMBARRASSMENT.
FAILURE.
EXCOMMUNICATION.
THE FOUR HORSEMEN
OF THE APOCALYPSE.**

Remember how we talked about silence being the most powerful presentation tool? Because it was such an incredible show of confidence to leave a gap where anyone could jump in?

Well, questions are the second most powerful tool. You are quite literally inviting the audience to jump in. They could say anything. Absolutely anything! It's MADNESS to take the chance.
WHAT ARE YOU THINKING?

Personally, I'm thinking that I have a trick for that. And now you will, too.

"THERE ARE NO BAD ANSWERS, ONLY BAD RECOVERIES!"

See, it turns out that with just a bit of planning, there's no such thing as the wrong answer.

Like Mike

I used to give a talk about the importance of learning through a program vs learning by experience. In it, I talked about a 5'5" high school basketball player who wanted to dunk. It went like this:

Everyday, for three hours, he would go out and try to dunk. He did this for a solid year. And after all that time, what do you think happened?

Most people said, *"He could dunk?"*

And I would happily shout, *"NO! Three hours a day, everyday, for a year straight, and he still couldn't dunk. But three months later, he could. Here's what changed…"* And then I would talk about how he discovered a weight lifting program that added eleven inches to his vertical leap.

But occasionally I'd get a pessimist in the audience. Once some smartass said, *"Well, I think you want me to say 'Yes' so I'm gonna say 'No'."*

To which I replied, *"THAT'S RIGHT. Three hours a day, everyday, for a year straight, and he still couldn't dunk. But three months later, he could. Here's what changed…"*

See? It didn't matter what the answer was. I was still able to direct their thinking towards what a waste a year of effort without specific guidance could be.

When done right, your questions will actually lead the client down a very narrow path. But because you're passing the mic, they feel as if they have total freedom.

It can be a bit of a brain teaser at first to figure out how to frame questions like this. But it's not even necessary every time, provided you know how to pivot from wrong answers.

STOP TALKING TO YOURSELF

START MAKING WRONG SEEM RIGHT

Your response to "wrong" answers should consist of two parts: acknowledging the participation (in essence, rewarding them for engaging) and pivoting to invite another answer.

Doing this smoothly removes the awkwardness of getting wrong answers. And all your audience remembers is how people wound up proving your point for you.

Here's a few ways to recover if the answers aren't quite what you expected.

- "We did see X sometimes. But actually, Y was the most common..."
- "That's interesting. What we've found though is..."
- "Good answer. There's an even better one, though..."
- "[Restate their answer]. What else?"
- "Y'know, we thought so too. But in fact…"

If there are multiple folks in the audience, you can acknowledge the wrong answer by repeating it back to them. Then canvass the room asking if there are any other answers until you find the one you want.

I use these constantly. It's always amusing to give a workshop about this topic and then ask people to think back to the beginning when I asked them questions and used these to find the answer I was looking for.

Well, it's amusing to me, at least.

Once you get the hang of it, these pivot phrases will dramatically transform how you feel about passing the mic mid-meeting:

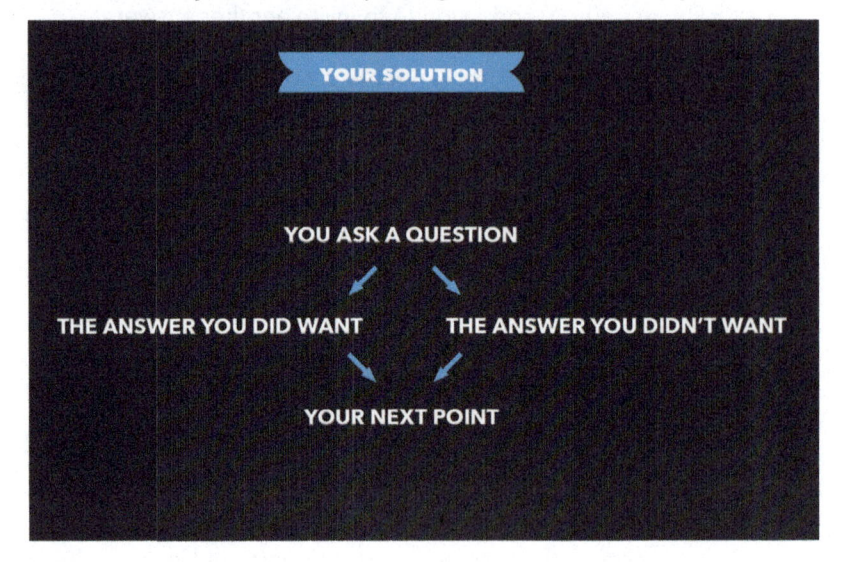

```
                    YOUR SOLUTION


                  YOU ASK A QUESTION

  THE ANSWER YOU DID WANT      THE ANSWER YOU DIDN'T WANT

                   YOUR NEXT POINT
```

Opinions are easy
This doesn't mean the answer has to be simple. But it shouldn't stump them. Asking about someone's opinion is easier than asking a question with one correct response. Sure, they may not give the "right" answer, but they won't really be "wrong" no matter what they say.

For example, asking them what their favorite food is will produce way more engagement than asking if anyone wants to guess the approximate population of Madagascar.

The one opinion you don't want to ask
Sometimes when people go to put this asking thing into practice, they say something like:

"So if we were to turn your ketchup into a superstar icon, what do you think that would look like?"

Asking the client to guess the impending solution actually checks all the boxes. It's opinion-based. It's not Yes/No. It's a pivotal moment.

Asking the client to guess the impending solution is also the worst thing you could possibly ask.

First, do not ask this because a client's first response (and it's a valid one) could be *"Um, isn't that what I'm paying you to tell me?"*

Second, do not ask this because they might answer it. And if the answer is different from yours (and it will be) you then have to quickly figure out how to make them love what you're about to say more than whatever they just said.

Think selling your best idea is hard? Try doing it after the client has eagerly pitched their concept of a skyscraper-sized ketchup bottle wrap of the Empire State Building.

Three things to make questions easier
Of all the concepts presented in this book, these engagement ones are likely the least intuitive. Both for you, and the client. So here are three things to increase your chances of success.

Expect this not to work
I mean, it'll work. I do it all the time. But it will be awkward as hell initially. We've trained clients for their entire careers to just sit back and be passive participants. You're going to need to teach them that they're expected to participate.

So anticipate the awkward silence when you start asking questions. It's ok. Hold that silence.

I've literally counted, "one one-thousand…two one-thousand…" in my head to reassure myself that it hasn't been six years since someone last spoke.

Under no circumstances should you answer for them. This is a game of verbal chicken, and you must win. When they break the silence, acknowledge and pivot.

Speaking of…

Don't talk for two
We creatives have a bizarre habit of asking rhetorical questions in presentations. Probably because we want to build (fake) suspense. Sometimes because we're fooling ourselves into believing that we gave the client a chance to participate. But it's a habit I need you to squash right now.

Asking a rhetorical question will prove to your audience that if they say nothing, you'll carry on without them. Since that's easier, they'll default to silence, making it even harder to engage them later.

So what do we do with rhetorical questions? We don't ask them.

(This is a book, not a presentation. Also, I did that on purpose.)

Don't hold up both ends of the conversation. Make them work.

I Lied To You Back There
Remember how I said no "Yes/No" answers? Well, I'll allow a few in the beginning. Questions like *"Can you see my screen?"* or *"Can everyone hear me?"* are an opportunity to train your client that you expect verbal responses.

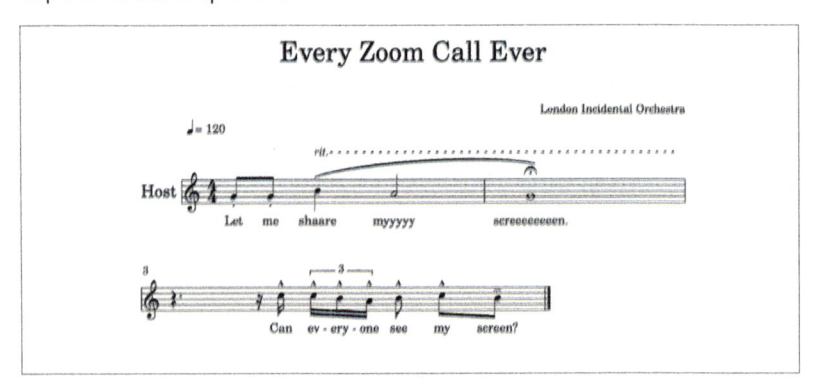

Every Zoom Call Ever — London Incidental Orchestra

(I don't know who made this, but I hope their Nobel Prize is in the mail).

STOP TALKING TO YOURSELF

> **From the window to the wall**
>
> When I'm in person, I always ask if the folks in the back can hear me.
>
> I'm not actually concerned about it. I project like a drill sergeant. I'm really just priming them to understand that when I ask a question, I expect a response.
>
> This is usually another moment in my workshops on engagement when folks feel manipulated. But they're willing to talk to me about it, so mission accomplished.

You can even start by asking for a show of hands, or some other "group" answer that encourages participation without singling anyone out.

Just remember that you can't answer for them. They have to do the work.

Remote note
Engagement is especially important if you're presenting remotely. Especially if you're presenting remotely to a bunch of folks who are "camera off."

You have no idea if they're tracking. If you have their focus. If they're even there. So ask questions. Make it a conversation as quickly as possible.

I've asked enough questions that folks have turned their cameras back on, feeling they needed to "be there" to participate in the conversation. I love to see how many faces I can make reappear by the end of a presentation.

Remember the importance of ½ time
It's hard to have a conversation if the other side doesn't have time to say anything. Don't neglect the rule of ½ time.

STOP FAILING YOUR FIRST IMPRESSION

Let's talk about the 3 mistakes you're probably making in the first 3 seconds of your meeting.

No, that's not a typo. I do mean the first three seconds.

13

START
MASTERING THE FIRST 3 SECONDS

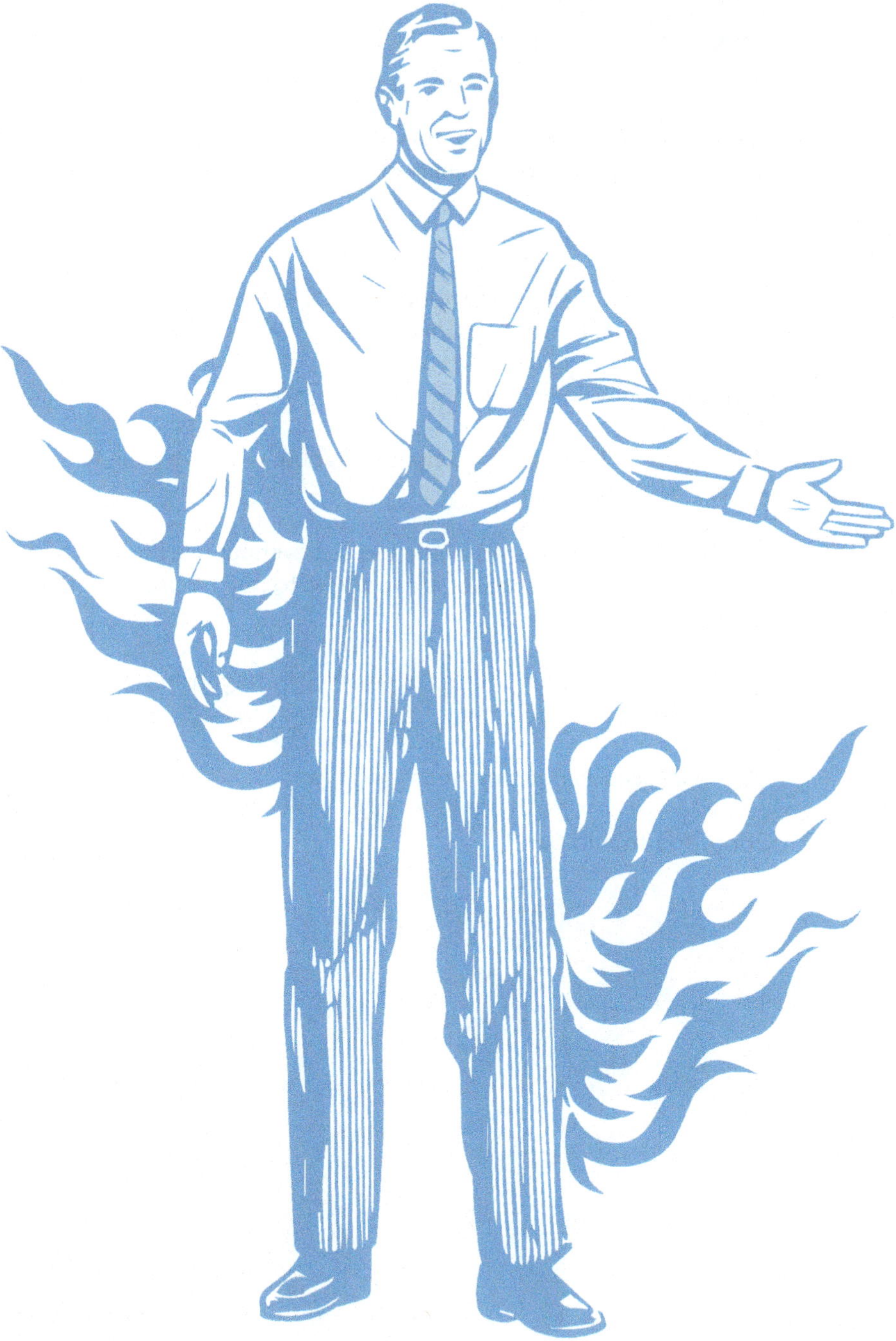

START OPENING WITH THE TRUTH

Fun fact: most creative presenters lie before they're even past the cover slide. And based on numbers alone, there's a good chance you're one of them.

Before you deny it, I have to tell you that these aren't big lies like *"I'm the King of Norway"* or *"This idea will 10X your ROI!"*

It's usually a tiny lie.

That lie, most often, is this: "We're really excited about the work we have to show you today."

This lie is usually delivered a little too fast, without eye contact, and quite often while the speaker is struggling to put the presentation up on screen.

That's right, the meeting hasn't even officially begun, and you've already lied.

"But I am excited about my work!" you cry.

Good. You should be.

But here's the issue: I don't believe you. And neither does your audience.

Imagine you gave someone a present. They open it, refuse to meet your eyes and deadpan, *"I'm really excited about this."*

Would you believe them?

Of course not. You would assume they're either trying to be funny, or lying.

So while you said, *"We're really excited,"* that's not what you're communicating.

Even if you didn't intend to, even if you weren't conscious of it, you just told your audience something that wasn't true. And it happens all the time.

In that moment, you taught your audience not to believe your words. You demonstrated they have to look past them to decipher the true intent of what you say.

If you're excited, let yourself feel it so that your audience can feel it. Don't just say the words- show the emotion.

Excitement is reflected in your face, in your body language, and in your eagerness to begin talking about the work instead of the weather, or the flight, or if anyone's hungry.

And when you're genuinely excited, it should come through in your language:

"Before we start, I just have to tell you that this has been an incredible opportunity."

"Teams were fighting to work on this project!"

"This one was really special to me, and I think you'll see why as we go through it."

Or (and I know this sounds crazy) say nothing. More than once I've stood smiling silently next to my laptop until the small talk died down and someone said, *"I think Ben wants to start."*

The Whole Truth

I once stood at the front of a room desperately excited about what we had to show. To the point where the only words I could think of were *"We are so excited to show this to you."*

But I knew the phrase was bankrupt. And so I took a breath and told an even more complete truth:

"Look, I'm not supposed to say this. Because we treat all our clients equally. And…we do. Really. But this project…I had to beat folks off this brief with a stick. They were volunteering to work on it after hours. This felt really special, and we're really excited about it."

And they could tell I meant every word.

STOP FAILING YOUR FIRST IMPRESSION

START USING INTERESTING COVER SLIDES

Here's every cover slide:

[Cover slide example: "COMPANY NAME x CLIENT NAME" with a sea turtle photo, "Project Name", and "DATE GOES HERE"]

What a massively missed opportunity. How? Let me count the ways:

- Project name
- Agency logo
- Client logo
- Today's date (Why? Who forgot what today's date was?)

As a meeting attendee, I know who I am, who you are, why I showed up, and (hopefully) today's date. There is not a single thing new here except, possibly, the photo. Which won't get nearly enough attention because you have four other elements distracting from it.

I mean, don't get me wrong, global warming is a much bigger issue than your cover slide. I'm just saying if you're planning to make a presentation about how to fix global warming, please don't make the cover slide look like this.

Challenge your audience's expectations or understanding. Signal that this meeting won't be like the forty-seven they sat through before it.

The bar for impactful cover slides is incredibly low. Half the time, I start with this:

Yes, really. This is incredibly effective. There are no distractions, and it doesn't pre-empt me. It lets me get my slideshow "ready" without giving away my opening, putting all of the focus on the presenter.

It's especially great if you have something poignant to ask or provocative to say.

If I can't find a strong image, this is how I start my pitches. It's a total power move. Serious BDE (Big Deck Energy).

Rated M

I opened a pitch to Xfinity with, "You're not competing with Verizon. You're competing with sex, violence, and dragons."

It was true, too. *Game of Thrones* was at the height of its popularity. If you wanted to stick in consumer's minds, you weren't competing with ads, you were competing with HBO.

Trust me, no one checks their phone during the meeting when you start out like that.

Here's another great way to start a presentation: full bleed imagery.

For example, this is the cover to my *Handling Objections* workshop:

I make sure to say nothing for a second after putting it up.

This technique can be especially powerful if paired with a strong line. For example, the first words out of my mouth after revealing this image are, *"Yes, we're about to rehash all your worst client trauma. If anyone would like to take a moment to set up an appointment with their therapist or drinking buddy, now's the time."*

Spoilers?

But your pitch could just as easily start with a representation of the client's challenges or successes.

I've said it before, I'm saying it again: the presentation is an ad for your ads. So open up with some emotion.

What is it they want most? Money? Power? Fame? Cut right to the heart of the matter.

For example, if I were pitching Samsung, I might open with an image of the line outside an Apple store. Of course, Samsung wants that outcome. So, they'll listen to how I think we can make that happen for them.

Of course, sometimes the right quote or statement will create the provocation you want to open with.

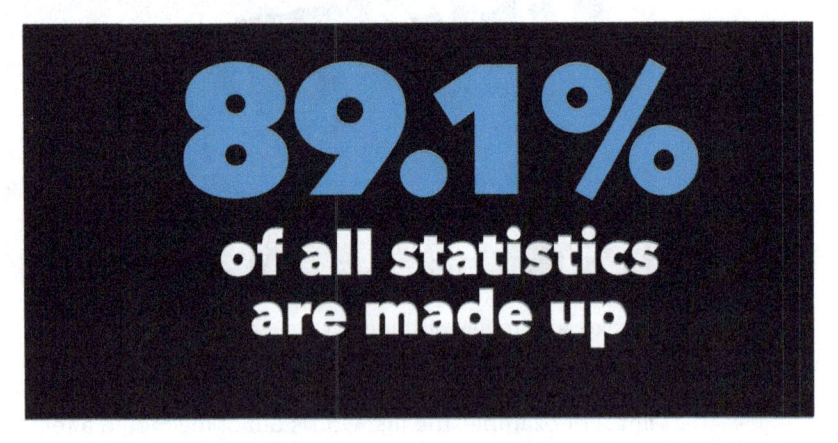

89.1%
of all statistics are made up

You might argue that this is just one slide. Everyone ignores the cover anyway. It's a silly detail.

But the cover is your first impression; your hook, and your chance to metaphorically give them an energy drink enema.

You can hope that the work will provide that when you get to it.

You can pray they'll see the benefits when you reach the end.

But why force them to overcome that first mundane impression? It's far easier to start strong and carry that energy through. And in my experience, it's far more successful.

So, whatever you do, don't start with the date.

STOP FAILING YOUR FIRST IMPRESSION

START OWNING THE SPOTLIGHT

Remember that whole rant I had a few chapters back around slides? About how you're the point of the presentation?

Well, now think about what happens when you share your screen in a presentation:

You quite literally minimize yourself.

Now everyone's staring at a giant, dumb slide- that probably says nothing significant — and you have no idea if they even see your thumbnail anymore.

It's the presentation equivalent of Homering into the bush:

And sure, you could argue this is only a problem when you're presenting virtually. But have you ever seen someone who spent the entire meeting with their back to the audience, speaking directly to their slide? Same thing, different method.

Do not minimize yourself. You're the focus. Maintain the spotlight.

This is why, in virtual meetings, I present like a weatherman.

I don't have a presentation deck. I have a series of virtual backgrounds. And I project them behind me as I go through the presentation.

Y'know, like a weatherman.

This way, I never have to worry about being minimized.

STOP FAILING YOUR FIRST IMPRESSION

When I want folks to focus on the slides, I just move out of frame.

CAN YOU SEE MY SCREEN?

When I want their attention again, I move back in front of the slides.

This is the same thing we'll talk about when we cover body language a bit further on.

Now I recognize that for a variety of reasons, not everyone is gonna go full weatherman. Maybe it's the tech. Or the agency has some weird mandate. Or your dog ate your green cyc.

But if you're stuck using slides virtually, the best thing you can do is get into the habit of spamming that share screen button off and on like you're throwing a lightswitch rave party.

Share the slides, but only as long as necessary. When you're speaking, get those things off the screen so the client can continue to build a relationship with you. Not your tiny/nonexistent thumbnail.

There's the three mistakes most people make in the first three seconds of their presentation. And what to do about them.

STOP WASTING YOUR LAST IMPRESSION

Let us assume that you've taken the initial lessons to heart, and you now end your presentations by discussing *How the World Will Be*.

But how do you literally finish the presentation? If the answer is with a slide that says, "Thank You," we're about to get in a fight.

14

START REPLACING "THANK YOU" SLIDES

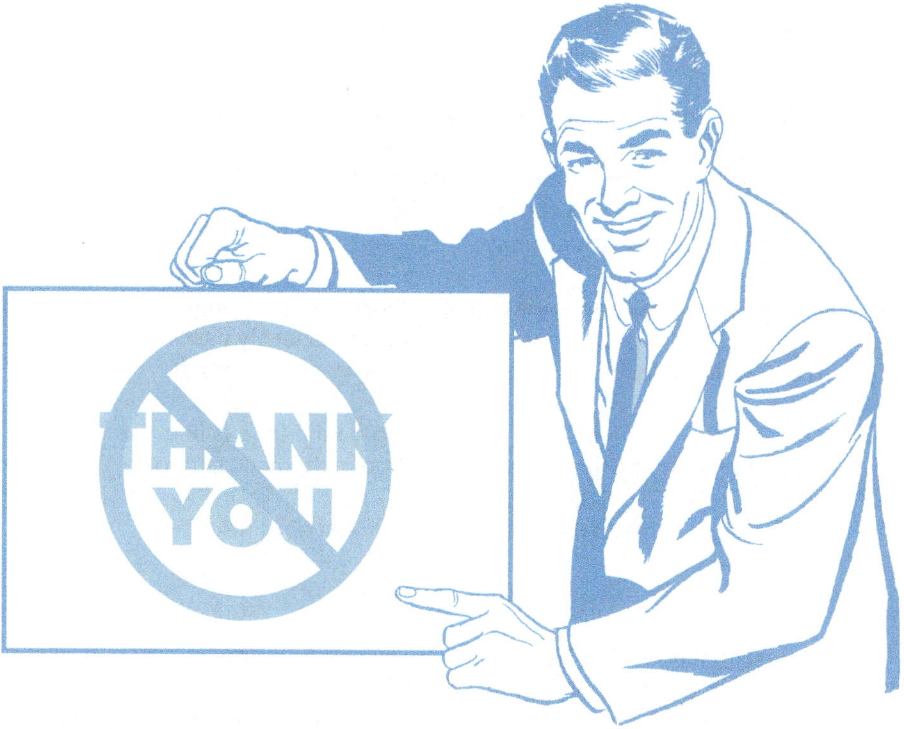
THANK
YOU

START REPLACING "THANK YOU" SLIDES

There are two kinds of presenters in the world: those who agree with me on this, and those who are wrong.

Look, it's really, really unusual that you are genuinely going to thank your client for the time they've given you. I mean, genuinely.

You can do it politely. You can do it because you think this is what you're supposed to do at this point or because you don't know how to end the presentation. But (just like when we talked about saying you're really excited at the start) you're rarely going to be genuinely grateful for the opportunity.

There's a kind of subservient message that comes with thank you. The king has allowed you to speak in their presence, and you are graciously thanking them for their time. It's a really bad vibe to set going into a round of feedback.

I would end on anything else. Ending on the logo is fine. I've gotten in the habit of writing the equivalent of a thematic sign-off.

Ending a sports pitch with *"And the crowd goes wild."*

An animated execution with *"That's all, folks."*

A sci-fi theme with *"To infinity! Or at least ComiCon!"*

Use something that is obvious as an endpoint, but not *"Thank you, your Highness. I appreciate the opportunity to speak to you."*

Don't give them that power.

And while you're at it…

STOP WASTING YOUR LAST IMPRESSION

START SIGNALING IT'S THEIR TURN TO SPEAK

There is a trick of film and stage that subtly indicates to the audience that the show is about to end and they should be prepared to applaud.

Applied correctly, this prevents any of those awkward silences where the client isn't quite sure you're done yet. Or a moment where you end almost too quickly and then are suddenly stuck looking around going, *"Thank you,"* or *"...That's it,"* before hurriedly sitting down and hoping somebody breaks the silence.

Here's the trick:

1. Slow your pacing
2. Soften your projection
3. Lower your pitch

If you do these three things, it is going to indicate to your audience that you are reaching the end of your presentation…

> that what you are currently talking about is the most important thing you want to end on…

> and that now-

> -it is their turn.

So you can be very excited about what you're talking about. You can share with them all kinds of knowledge, all kinds of thoughts about *How the World Will Be* (since that's how you're ending, right?) And then, as you reach your final point, you bring the plane in for a landing.

START MEMORIZING

WHAT?

"Ben, you had a whole rant at the start of this book that no one should ever memorize. Ever. What the hell do you mean 'Start memorizing'??!?"

I never advocate memorization. Ever.

If you try to memorize, you're going to be searching for the next word mid-presentation when you should be focusing on your audience and creating a natural flow between your points.

So never do it.

Except in two places.

Your opening thoughts. And your closing ones.

Nerves most commonly hit in the beginning of a presentation. Memorizing your first few lines means you'll be able to say them on autopilot if you need a few seconds to collect yourself.

It also means you won't risk any "Uh…um" at the start, since you'll know exactly what words you want to say.

STOP WASTING YOUR LAST IMPRESSION

The end of your presentation is like the final note in a song. At worst, it should feel thoughtful. At best, it should take everything that came before it to new heights. I've seen a mediocre presentation saved by a strong, convincing sign off at the buzzer.

So don't leave that last impression to chance. Know exactly how you want to finish your presentation, and make sure you know it going into the room.

If you don't? Put that final thought right on the slide.

It'll beat the hell out of "Thank you".

STOP BELIEVING NERVES

Helping people conquer nerves is one of my favorite things about being a presentation coach.

Because I know just how terrible nerves can be.

I've been so nervous I've hallucinated sensations.
So nervous my mouth dried up and my lips chapped.
So nervous I had to stand on one foot because the other was shaking too badly.

And I'm far from alone.

I've worked with folks who couldn't speak without anti-anxiety meds. Folks who broke down and apologized mid-presentation. Folks who blacked out during their pitch, with no idea of what they just said.

Folks who screamed like the end of *Shawshank Redemption* because they couldn't take the nerves.

And I was able to help each and every one of them.

You should know- there's going to be a lot of science in this section. That's because nerves are crafty little devils who will completely warp our perception of reality. And if we can't rely on our own senses, the building blocks of the universe are the next best things.

I can't promise a single chapter is going to banish your nerves. But here's a few tips you can use to lessen their impact.

START UNDERSTANDING NERVES AREN'T REAL

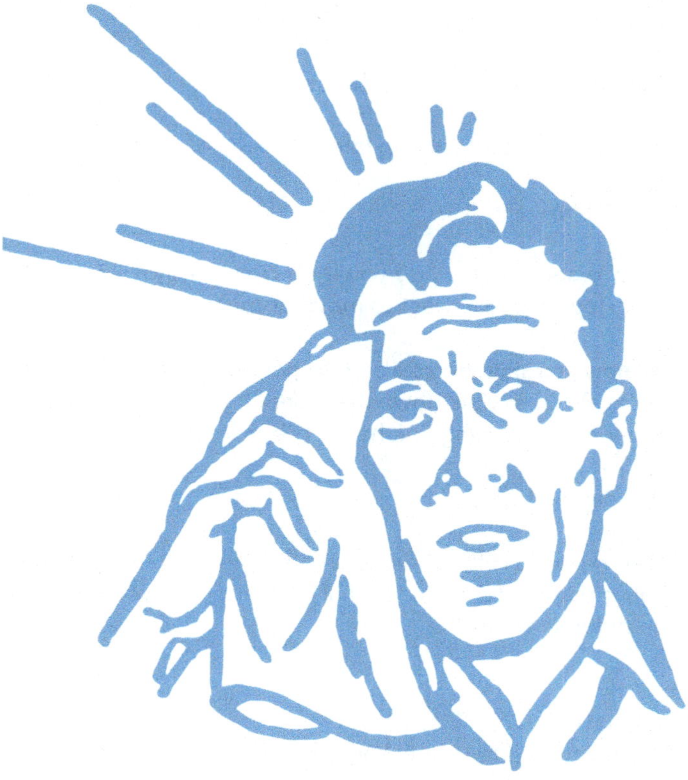

START UNDERSTANDING NERVES AREN'T REAL

Like Santa, the Tooth Fairy, and honest politicians, nerves aren't real.

That's right. You're making them up.

What we call nerves are an interpretation of adrenaline.

Here, I'll prove it:

If you're nervous, how do you feel? Heart racing? Short of breath? Shaky legs, like you want to move or run or jump around?

Ok, now imagine you're about to get on a roller coaster. Or maybe you're about to walk down the aisle. Or you're receiving a big award. Or a friend is coming you haven't seen for a long time.

How do you feel?

Heart racing? A little short of breath? Are you talking louder, faster, higher pitched? Do you feel full of energy, like you want to move or run or jump around?

Exactly.

Adrenaline is adrenaline. Your body doesn't know whether you're excited or terrified. Your mind chooses to interpret those signals one way or another.

STOP BELIEVING NERVES

All you have to do is reinterpret your response.

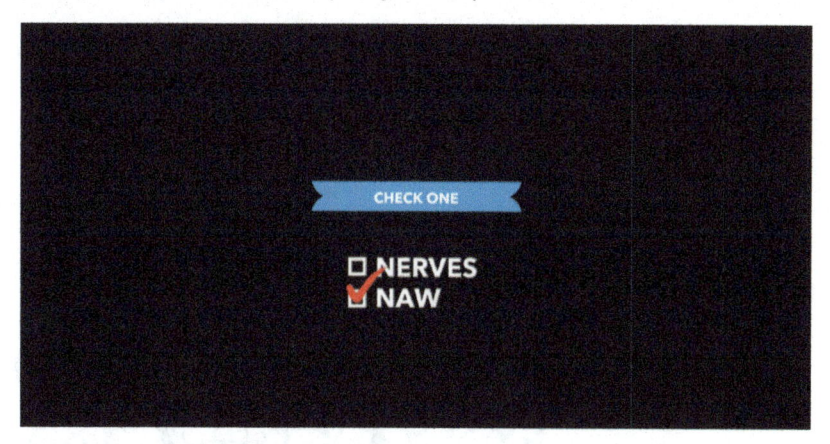

```
                    CHECK ONE

                    ☐ NERVES
                    ✓ NAW
```

Tell yourself that your symptoms mean you're ready for this presentation and that you're excited to put all that thought and effort into practice.

I know. It can't be that simple, right? But I've had clients virtually extinguish their nerves after using this hack four or five times. It really can change that quickly.

Adrenaline is a biological response. But nerves are a choice.

Olympic Optimism

A study was done of nearly 100 Olympic athletes. People whose four years of training came down to a single moment.

They were asked, *"When you step up to that starting line, or diving block, or balance beam—are you nervous?"*

Every answer was the same. *"I'm not nervous. I'm excited."*

START MANIPULATING THE CLOSED LOOP

When it comes to adrenaline, your physiology is a closed loop.

That's science-talk for "What happens to your body affects your mind, and vice versa".

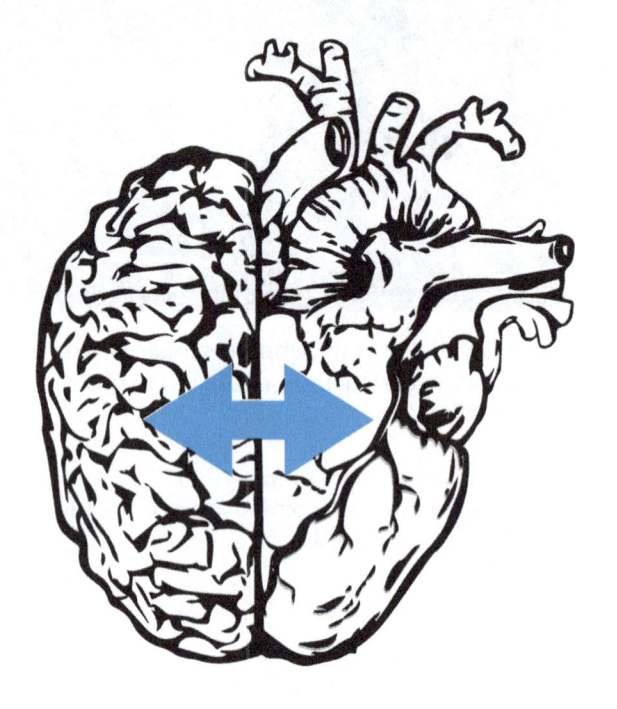

The bad news is that if your heart starts to race, your brain will go "WHY IS THE HEART RACING? SOUND THE ALARM, WE MUST BE UNDER THREAT!"

STOP BELIEVING NERVES

If your brain thinks, "MAN, I DO NOT WANT TO BE PRESENTING RIGHT NOW. THEY'RE ALL GONNA LAUGH AT ME," your heart will prepare for warp speed because it reacts like you're in physical danger.

But the bad news is also the good news. And the worse news is even better news.

If whatever affects one half also affects the other half, focusing on one part can lessen your nerves overall.

So if you have an easier time talking yourself off mental ledges, focus on your mental state. Calm that, and your physical symptoms will go away as well.

If you find it easier to control your body, then work on things like breathing. And as you relax your body your mind will follow.

Choose whichever path feels easier in the moment.

START CONTROLLING YOUR MIND

Reinterpreting adrenaline symptoms is one way to control your mind. Pretty soon, you won't need to consciously think about it at all. You'll just start to recognize those symptoms as excitement for what's coming up (your meeting).

Another way to quiet your mind is to trust that your symptoms don't transmit to the audience in even a fraction of the way they feel to you.

I know this sounds too good to be true. But in my experience it isn't just true- it's *universally* true.

A few stories to make this point.

Jump scare

Early on in my coaching career, I was running a small group workshop. A young developer was presenting. She'd professed to having terrible nerves, but she was doing really well. No trembling, no hesitation in her speech, no shakiness in her voice...she was doing great.

Without warning, she suddenly threw back her head and SCREAMED. It was like a combination of *Point Break* and *Poltergeist*. Everyone in the room jumped.

"I'm sorry," she said breathlessly, "I just couldn't take it. It was so bad."

Not a single one of us could tell she was struggling. Internally, she had been dealing with an emotional hurricane. Outwardly? We never even felt a breeze.

One more.

Two truths and a lie

My second day at a new agency, I was invited to do "something" during an all-agency meeting to introduce myself. I decided to read a children's book that I wrote and illustrated for my son.

But that morning the nerves hit almost immediately. Still, I tried to power through. Doing all the voices, showing the pictures after I read each page, the whole thing.

Luckily, we were all sitting in a circle on the floor, so my usual leg shaking wasn't immediately visible. But about halfway through, the tremors became so bad I literally elbowed the guy next to me. I felt the contact.

Now, here's the kicker: someone had recorded it and put the whole thing on social media.

Dreading what I would see (but committed to watching myself on camera to inject some reality into my impressions) I watched the clip. I was looking specifically for the part where I elbowed my new coworker.

It never happened.

I don't mean it wasn't as bad as I thought. I mean it literally never took place. I watched that thing 3x through. I was pausing frames. My arm never jumped. I had no visible tremors. The entire thing was in my head. My panic manufactured the sensations.

This is why I trust in science, not impressions. Over and over, I watch as people who swear they were nervous look perfectly calm. Your nerves do not show in the same degree to which you feel them.

And remember that it's not a bit of a racing heart or racing thoughts that are the problem. It's the toilet-bowl-flushing spiral of doom that gets worse and worse until you break to a point where it does become obvious.

Like that developer who screamed.

So if you start to feel nervous, take comfort in the truth that no one else can see yet. And start to use the exercises here to settle down.

PRACTICE EXERCISE:
FACE YOURSELF

What you'll need:

- Something to present
- A way to record yourself

What you'll do

Record yourself presenting. It doesn't have to be long. Five to ten minutes are just fine. The hard part is what comes next.

Watch yourself.

None of us want to do this. It's awful. Uncomfortable. You spend a lot of time going, *"Oh I don't do that- why do I do that?"*

Which is why it's such a great tool. There's a few things here you should look for specifically:

- Where are you looking? Some people have a habit of speaking while looking off to the side.
- What's your thinking face? We all have one. Most people look up or down when searching for a word. Just recognize yours.
- Do you have a tic? Some people scratch their neck, nose, or cheek. It's totally unconscious, but can be very distracting.
- What are you doing with your hands? Do you wave them around a lot? Are they too close to the camera? Do they cross in front of your face? (Hint: don't put them in front of your face.)

If you see yourself doing all or some of these, know you're not alone. The goal is to be more aware of your behavior when presenting, so you can begin to change it if you need to.

START CONTROLLING YOUR BODY

I feel like most people know about box breathing at this point. If you don't, a quick search will bring you up to speed on the most popular breathing technique for combatants and first responders.

It's great, and it obviously works. But there are two other techniques I prefer to use to gain quick control over my physical nervous symptoms.

Start being a dog
Science has proven the most effective way to calm your heart (and therefore your breathing, pulse, and nerves) is by doing the following:

1. Deep inhale (almost as much air as you can hold).
2. One more, tiny inhale of air (you should be almost bursting).
3. Looooooong exhale through your mouth.

And your heart rate should be noticeably slower in 1-2 seconds.

STOP BELIEVING NERVES

Oh, and if you don't believe me, believe dogs. They do this exact thing before settling down for a nap.

Start relaxing your hands
When we get nervous, we tense up. This impacts how we move, sound, and breathe during a presentation.

Of course, if you try to focus on un-tensing muscles in a stressful situation, you're probably not going to make much progress. Especially things like your shoulders or neck.

This is doubly true if you're attempting to do it while convincing your client that the entire concept will only work if it's shot on-site. In Hawaii. During golden hour. And that the logo should remain the size that it is.

But here's a fun fact: it's hard to remain tense if your hands are loose. Not impossible. But really hard.

Most of us have way more control over our hands than our neck muscles. So if you want to start to relax, start by releasing the death grip.

Please note- relaxed hands is the key here, as opposed to simply "not fists." Rigamortis Claws are not fists, but they are not calming whatsoever.

STOP STANDING AWKWARDLY

Alternate titles to this chapter were:

STOP STANDING LIKE A PALACE GUARD
(Ramrod straight because you're afraid to make the wrong movement, and so you make none whatsoever.)

STOP STANDING LIKE A BOUNCER
(Arms crossed. For those times when you want to make the client feel as uncomfortable as you do. And of course, there's The Bouncer's close relative: The Double Cross, where you cross your arms and legs.)

STOP STANDING LIKE AN INVISIBLE JUGGLER
(When you engage in circus-act-level arm waving. If your audience can easily imagine flaming torches or buzzing chainsaws as part of your point, you've got a problem.)

STOP STANDING LIKE A SHOPLIFTER
(Hands deep in your pockets. The polar opposite to the Juggler, but nearly as distracting. What are you hiding, exactly?)

STOP DOING THE SHIMMY
(Nothing says "Do they really need to pee? Or are they practicing for a dance number?" quite like swiveling your body left and right while standing or sitting in a meeting.)

STOP IMITATING A CAGED PANTHER
(When somebody continues to prowl left and right while speaking without once standing still. What in god's name did you take before this meeting? And can I have some of it the next time I'm tired?)

STOP SITTING LIKE MR BURNS
(Elbows on the table, fingertips touching. Acceptable only when threatening government leaders from an subterranean lair.)

The point is, there's an almost infinite number of ways we fail to stand normally. A good start is to simply stop doing any of the above.

START STANDING NATURALLY

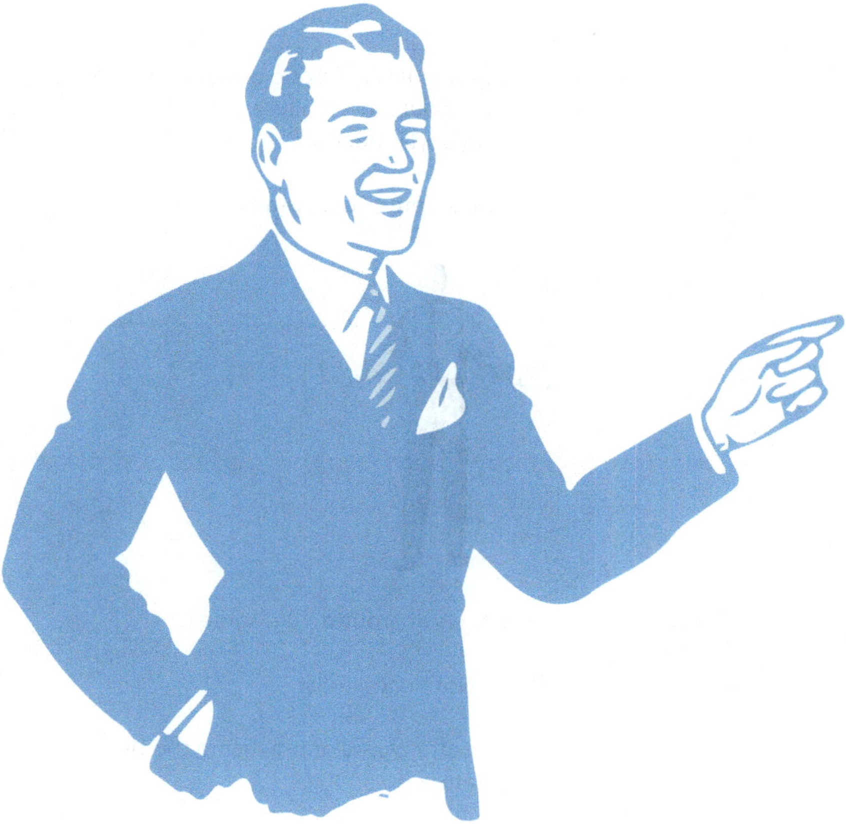

START STANDING NATURALLY

Talking about body language is like talking about breathing or blinking. You never think about it normally, and the second you start thinking about it is the second it becomes unnatural.

Still, there is a generally accepted "best practice" position for presenters. It's this:

Face your audience, elbows at around 90 degrees.

Isn't that easy? Well, no. Not necessarily.

That is best practice. And after years of practicing the best practice, it's how I tend to stand naturally.

But this can come off just as awkward as any of the behaviors described on the previous page.

If you adopt the best practice position and then freeze like a deer in the headlights, you'll look like you're cosplaying C-3PO.

Which is why I think the most important aspect of standing naturally is to move. Naturally.

I've seen folks stand with their arms crossed, but frequently uncross them and gesture to their audience. That doesn't seem nearly as closed off as most speakers. (I still don't want you to do this. I'm just making a point.)

STOP STANDING AWKWARDLY

Use this as a guide, not a law. The most important thing is to try and act natural. Make sure you're shifting your weight without shimmying. Make sure you're using your hands without juggling. If you catch yourself going too far in one direction or another, just correct.

In short, start by becoming aware of your typical motions and stances, and then start to add the best practices in.

START PLAYING SIMON SAYS IN MEETINGS

Fun fact about humans: we're programmed to track movement. This is because, evolutionarily speaking, it was very important to know whether or not that movement was being made by a hungry lion.

We don't stop doing this in meetings, even though few lions make it to the C-suite. That means that you can use your body language to direct your audience's attention.

If you stand to the side of your slides and gesture or glance at them, folks in the room will automatically look where you're looking or gesturing.

Similarly, if you want them to focus on you, you can start to move around more. I usually take a few steps to stand in front of my slides. They literally can't continue to read them—a pretty clear sign I'd like their attention.

"NOW BACK TO ME..."

STOP STANDING AWKWARDLY

START SITTING STRATEGICALLY

Yes, you can sit wrong in meetings. I don't mean physically wrong like "sitting on the table instead of the chair" or "putting your feet up on the table." I mean sitting in a location that makes your audience work harder.

Choosing to be at the head of the table furthest from the screen means that your audience has to constantly turn back and forth between the screen and you. It will make them feel like they're sitting midcourt at a tennis tournament.

Don't give your audience whiplash. Sit near your slides.

Standing room only

Never be afraid to adjust yourself or the room to make things more comfortable for your audience.

I was planning to lead a concepting session with a client where I'd stand at the white board, ask questions, and write the answers. But the room was a little smaller than expected, and when the client sat down they were basically six inches from my belt buckle.

New plan: I sat in a chair to ask the questions, then stood up to write the answers before returning to my seat. That way I avoided lording over the client.

START AVOIDING GIFs

Our focus on motion is why I generally avoid GIFs in slide presentations. Unless used with extreme care, the constant motion will overpower your presence. I have seen exactly one agency use GIFs in a way that felt additive to the presentation. They know who they are. Odds are you are not them. I recommend steering clear of GIFs.

If you must use a GIF, make sure you have a follow up slide with just a freeze frame of it. Something static that won't upstage you.

And just in case a few of you aren't mad enough at me after reading that last paragraph- it's pronounced GIF like "gift." Hard G. I don't care what the original programmer said. What were we talking about again?

START STARING APPROPRIATELY

Let's talk about the windows to the soul, shall we?

The best presenters make people feel as though they're being spoken to directly. Those questions we covered earlier? They're a great way to do that. Another way? Look at the people you're talking to.

Like standing normally, this is a perfectly ordinary act that many people struggle to do in meetings. So let's run through some DO's and DON'Ts.

Don't
Stare at one person exclusively- especially without blinking- as if they're the only person in the room. You're presenting, not proposing. Also? This makes everyone else feel like they're not important and they'll tune you out.

STOP STANDING AWKWARDLY

Do
Spread your gaze around the folks assembled. Because good leaders will see how you address their team. Plus, odds are you'll be speaking to those team members more than those leaders.

Don't
Madly scan from one person to the next like a half-starved honey badger trying to find its next meal.

Do
Shift your gaze during natural breaks in speech. For example, you can shift it from one person to another where you would hear the comma in a sentence. Or at the end of a point. Doing it in the middle of a phrase will make you appear a bit frantic.

Don't
Overthink the above and panic that you've looked at someone for too long and immediately glance away as soon as you look at them. That comes across as dismissive, and super insulting. In eye language, it reads as, "Oh, not you." If you catch yourself back on the same person too soon, just finish the thought and then try the other side of the room.

Do
Remember to blink occasionally.

STOP MAKING VIRTUAL MEETINGS HARDER

Virtual meetings are hard. They minimize your strengths and magnify your weaknesses.

Got great voice modulation? Not anymore. Between your mic and their speakers, your voice could sound like Mickey Mouse, and you'd have no idea.

Find it difficult to sit still? Now that you're in a closeup, all those little movements become big distracting ones.

Have a client with shrinking attention spans? They'll just "multitask" off camera and tune you out entirely.

Technology, amirite?

A lot of the rules are the same no matter how you're presenting (don't swivel in your chair, don't pass your hands in front of your face). But there are three things you can do to improve your body language when no bodies are actually present for your presentation.

Think lights, camera, angles.

Controlling these three elements of your remote setup will take you from amateur to news-anchor-level professional. Or at least give you a better shot at keeping the client's attention.

START
CONTROLLING YOUR LIGHTING

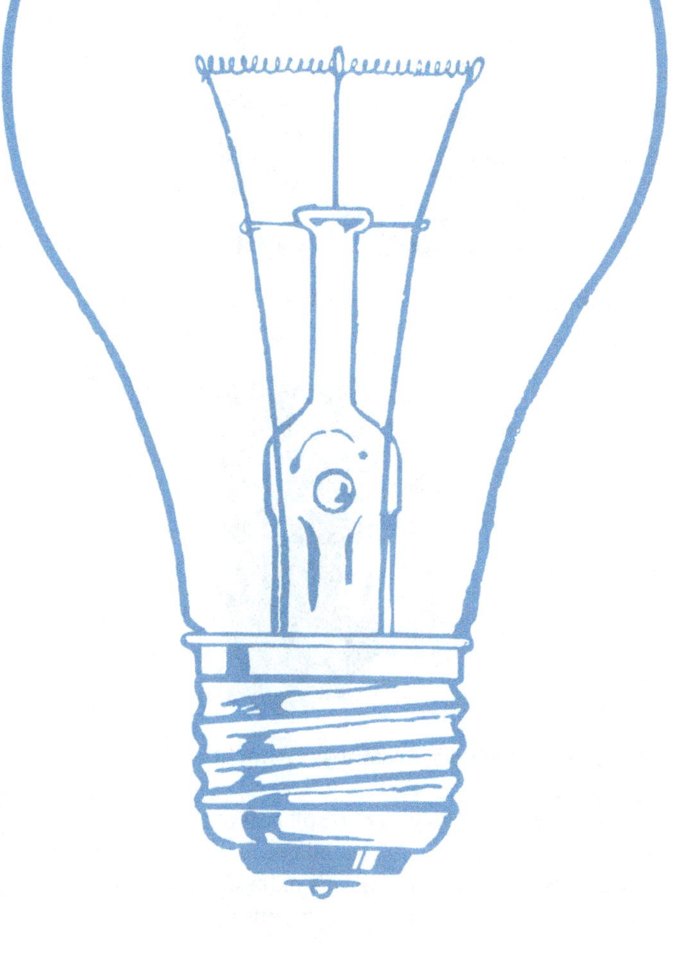

START CONTROLLING YOUR LIGHTING

Bad illumination will sink a meeting faster than almost anything else. Look at this guy:

"LOOK INTO THE LIGHT!"

He looks like he's two seconds from being Raptured. And then there's this one…

"THEY'LL NEVER FIND ME!"

…who looks like he's in Witness Protection.

In the first case while you can still make out some of his face, it's not easy. So you're losing almost all the facial cues that make a video call useful in the first place. Plus, it's exhausting for the audience to stare into a bright light for an entire meeting.

In the second case, John Doe there might as well be pixelated for all the information you can read from his expression.

224

I'm no Director of Photography, but here's a simple hack to fix your lighting: make sure the brightest light in the room is behind your webcam. This will illuminate your face first, and make the background a bit dark in comparison. Perfect to bring you into focus for your audience.

Keep in mind the brightest light source could come from a window. If it is, your light balance will need to be adjusted throughout the day.

START SPEAKING TO CAMERA

If you speak directly to your camera, your audience will feel as though you're speaking directly to them. But that's actually easier said than done.

One of the fun little ironies of presenting virtually is that when you're looking at your audience, you're not looking at your webcam.

Which means that, from the perspective of your audience, you're looking anywhere but them.

We all know why this happens. But on some level our brains still interpret this as a lack of interest, or honesty, or importance. It's a massive barrier to building a relationship with your audience over video.

STOP MAKING VIRTUAL MEETINGS HARDER

The next thing you want to do is collect your audience as high up toward the top of your screen (and your webcam) as possible. That way when you look at them, you're practically looking into the webcam. Boom. Virtual eye contact.

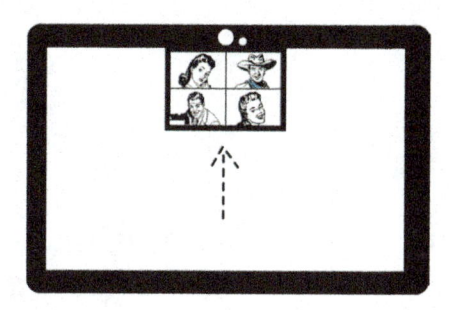

START OWNING YOUR ANGLES

Speaking of screens, most of us are used to them sitting on a desk at a quite serviceable angle like so:

Nothing wrong with that. Except if you're trying to look into your camera, as we discussed, you're going to wind up with a double chin. Also, the slightly lower viewing angle can result in history's greatest unintentional fashion faux pas.

My friends, I give you the ceiling fan hat.

It's incredible how many times I see this in meetings. Sometimes, they're even turned on, which is so much better.

But it's not just fans. Items left on bookshelves appear to sit on shoulders. Potted plants grow out of heads. The fun is practically endless.

At this point, some people might start complaining about how they work out of a studio apartment that would make Harry Potter's room under the stairs look like the Taj Mahal.

That's fine. Just make sure your background is clean. If that's your bed, make sure it's made for the client meeting. And don't leave your pajamas out. It's distracting.

If all else fails, blur your background. The filter exists for a reason.

Most people have spent time finding a "working" arrangement for their tech, where their computer is in a position most convenient for typing, glare is off the screen, and they sit comfortably.

What you need to consider is a "presenting" arrangement as well. Something that won't take you hours to set up, but raises your laptop, takes into account the lighting, and works with your background.

These days, I have a standing desk on wheels and various lights set up around my office. But in the beginning, I just had a stack of board games I used to shove under my laptop to get the built in webcam at eye level. Don't overthink it. But do think it.

PRACTICE EXERCISE:
BACKGROUND BLINDNESS

Catching these mistakes is tricky to do on your own, because we all become used to our surroundings very quickly. Our lazy brains (yup, still the issue) have a tendency to ignore things that don't move in our peripheral vision.

You're literally at a biological disadvantage here.

Best thing to do? Call up a friend and ask them if anything behind you is distracting, out of place, or unintentional clothing.

But try to use someone who hasn't seen your setup a hundred times already.

STOP GETTING STUMPED

Over and over again, I hear creatives say one of their biggest fears is getting caught speechless in meetings.

Maybe the client asks a question they didn't see coming. Or they realize there's a massive typo on the slide mid-pitch, and aren't sure how to handle it. Or their mind just draws a blank.

Some of the most absurd meeting behaviors I've ever seen have been the result of a momentary freeze. Folks will laugh maniacally. They'll beg forgiveness. They'll try to pass off lies so absurd a child could see through them.

At the same time, I've lost track of how many people have complimented me on always knowing just what to say. Or how "quick" I am in meetings. It's often one of the first things people comment on when the meeting is done.

I'm about to reveal how I improvise so well in meetings. (Spoiler alert: It's not natural ability) And how you can keep from ever being struck speechless again.

START PREPARING TO IMPROVISE

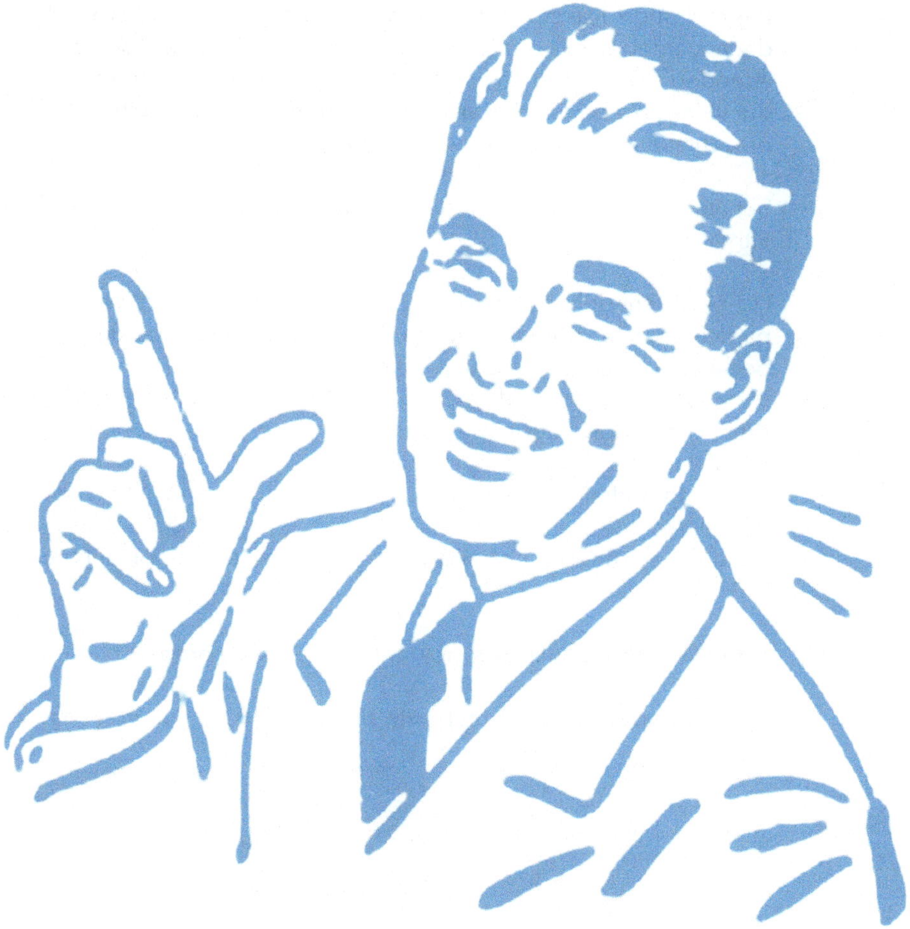

Improvisation, like storytelling, is a word that gets thrown around a decent amount in creative departments. It usually means somebody attended a workshop on how to use "Yes, and" in brainstorming. But it can also be used as an excuse: *"I don't need to practice the presentation; I'm better when I just improv."*

But when I think of improvisation in a meeting, I'm not thinking of either usage.

I've established (hopefully) that a good presentation involves participation from your audience. That can be nerve-wracking, because your audience is unpredictable.

What if they don't laugh at your jokes?

What if they challenge your argument?

What if they show up late and you have to deliver your presentation in 30 seconds?

In the face of the unknown, how can you possibly prepare?

The key is to develop comfort with situations where you don't have total control.

STOP GETTING STUMPED

This uncertainty isn't unique to the conference room.

Consider professional athletes. They can't know exactly what the other side will do, but they plan for as many eventualities as possible. Then, they train to develop the reflexes and skills necessary to remain as adaptable as they can be. As a presenter, you can do the same.

Don't like sports? Jazz musicians practice scales constantly, despite the fact that they never know what notes they'll play when the music starts. Why? So that they're ready regardless of what chords come their way. Presenters can do likewise.

To develop strong presentation reflexes, you need to do three things:

1. Control what you can
2. Anticipate what you can't
3. Practice your best-case responses to worst-case scenarios

One of a kind

If I had a dollar for every time I heard a CD tell me "We can't sell that," I'd be typing this from my private Island, sipping aged rum and getting my feet nibbled by tiny fishes. (It's a thing, look it up.)

But only once in my career did a CD listen to my proposed pitch and reply, *"Ok. And what will you do if they say 'No'?"*

That moment changed my career. It made me realize that we don't need to walk into meetings with our fingers crossed, our lucky socks, and whispered prayers on our lips.

We can plan for the less-than-best scenario.

Before you start hyperventilating about all the things that could go wrong, let's run through a quick list of just some of what you can control:

- Your attire
- Your content
- Your strategy
- Your preparation
- Your slides
- Your opening statement
- Your body language
- Your questions to the audience
- Your response to the audience's questions

Over the years, I have been accused of being quick on my feet. Of having magic powers. Of always knowing exactly what to say.

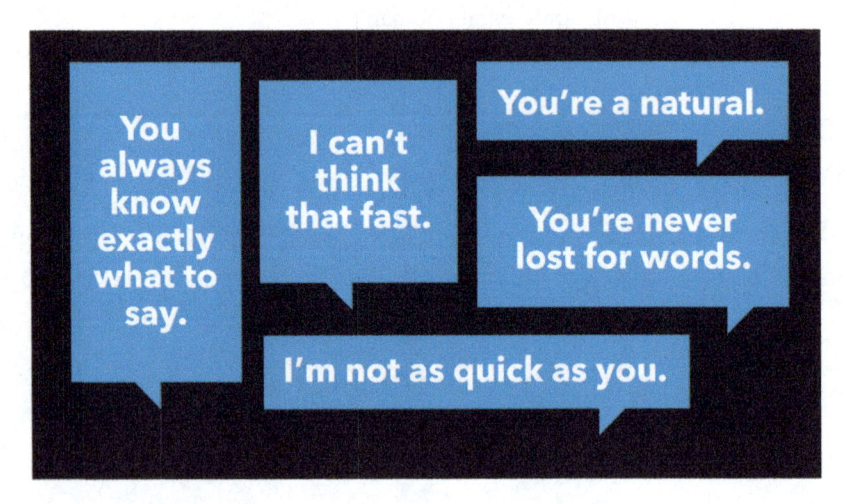

STOP GETTING STUMPED

And that's just off the top of my head. My point is, it's not like you're putting on a blindfold and jumping off a cliff. You can absolutely stack the deck in your favor. (Pun very much intended)

I have handled difficult clients so well over the phone that after we hung up, my coworkers spontaneously applauded as if I had just performed a magic trick.

Which actually wasn't far off. It wasn't luck or natural ability. It was a specific kind of preparation.

Or to put it another way, it is exactly like magic. A trick. A feint. A presentation sleight-of-hand. And once you know the trick, you can do it too. The secret is what I call *The Oh Sh*t Toolkit*. Let's build yours together.

PRACTICE EXERCISE:
FEARLIST
(SEE WHAT I DID THERE?)

I want you to think about the ten worst things that could happen to you during a meeting. Yes, ten.

It could be personal (e.g., "I forgot what I was saying").

It could be logistical (e.g., "My slides don't work").

It could be in your mind (e.g., "I feel like people are laughing at me").

These are the things that keep you up at night in a cold sweat the day before a presentation:

1. _____
2. _____
3. _____
4. _____
5. _____
6. _____
7. _____
8. _____
9. _____
10. _____

Did you struggle to get to ten? Over the years it seems like most people run out of fears around the 6-8 mark. Oh, your mind has created infinitely detailed and specific variations of how your tech might fail in a meeting, but at the end of the day, that's just a single fear.

Ok, now I want you to visualize each of those things happening to you. Really put yourself in the moment. If you do this right, you're going to feel extremely uncomfortable.

What if they hate it?

A lot of people fear a client's objections and critiques more than anything else. There's actually an entirely different lesson for that (it's got a sequence to follow and everything).

For now, just focus on all the other unexpected things that can happen during a presentation. We'll get to that other one soon enough.

STOP GETTING STUMPED

START BUILDING YOUR "OH SH*T" TOOLKIT

Now, choose one of those bowel-loosening moments from the previous list. I want you to think about what you wish you could do in that scenario (besides preventing it from ever happening).

What's the best-case response you could have? Can you think of a witty line? The perfect apology? A killer bon mot?

Ever been struck speechless in the moment? Then hours later, usually as you're about to fall asleep, you sit bolt upright and think *"That's what I should have said!"*

Yeah. That. That's what you're looking for. Only instead of figuring it out days later, you're gonna develop it days in advance.

You might not like what you come up with at first. It could even take several tries to get something you don't hate. That's ok. That's why we're doing it here, now, in a safe space.

But once you figure out what it is, go back to that uncomfortable worst-case-scenario, and run it through your mind again. This time, say your response out loud.

Practice it over and over again, until it becomes second nature. Just like those pro athletes who practice the same shot for hours until it becomes reflex.

Example 1: Speech-less
Some people fear nothing more than winding up speechless. I had a client whose *"Oh Sh*t"* response was *"...I just lost my place. Too bad they don't make Google maps for my brain."* That bought him enough time to recover. And more importantly, to do so without panicking.

Example 2: Tech, no babble

I often screw up transitioning from slides to video and back in meetings. When I inevitably display my desktop or a blank black square I say something like *"Sorry, I've clearly angered the internet gods today. Let me try a few more ritual sacrifices on my end, and if that doesn't work, I may have to restart the share."*

Ok, so I won't be getting my own stand up special anytime soon. But it's a damn sight better than, *"Umm, uhh, I'm not sure what's happening, sorry…uhhh."* Now a scenario I used to dread becomes perfectly manageable, thanks to my reflexive response about angry internet gods.

The goal with these responses is not to erase the problem, but to show that it hasn't thrown you.

At a base level, your goal is just to show you're not panicking. And because you're not nervous, your audience doesn't need to be either.

Believe it or not, a confident recovery can look even better than a "perfect" delivery. After all, nobody likes perfectionists. But we all appreciate someone who makes the save after a near-fumble.

STOP GETTING STUMPED

Whip smart

I once saw a live act where the performer demonstrated this perfectly. He was attempting to light a cigarette in someone's mouth- using an eight foot bullwhip.

He cracked the whip, and nothing happened.

"The first one is to build suspense." He said, to laughter from the audience.

He cracked the whip again, and nothing happened.

"The second is to build the suspense higher." More laughs.

"The third one-"

He cracked the whip again… and again nothing happened.

"-really pisses me off!"

The audience laughed uproariously, but I caught a slight change in his delivery.

That third miss wasn't part of the act. In fact, I'm not sure the second miss was either.

But he had an *Oh Sh*t Toolkit* for when things didn't happen right. And even though it didn't make the mistake go away, it let us know that the show was still going on.

The fourth time, he lit the cigarette. To thunderous applause.

In your own words
You want to ensure you're creating something you could say out loud that sounds like you. Otherwise, you'll make an awkward moment even more awkward.

Also, there's no one answer to these. Everyone's will sound different, and it may even come out differently each time. That's ok. The magic is not in the words themselves, but in having a phrase (reflex) to fall back on.

So even if the words change slightly, you know what to say.
Even if, like this person, you've forgotten what to say.

Off the ledge

I was running a workshop on this topic and asked the attendees about their greatest fears. One writer said, *"My greatest fear is when I… it's like I'm thinking and…,"* then suddenly exploded in frustration, *"This! This right here! I walk myself off a verbal cliff and have no idea how to get back!"*

In the silence that followed I replied, *"Actually, I think that would work pretty well."*

Two weeks later I was in a meeting with him where he lost his train of thought. *"Sorry, I just walked myself off a verbal cliff there, give me a second to get back on solid ground."*

He took a pause as the room waited politely. *"Ok, here's what I wanted to say…"*

START SAYING THIS WHEN YOU DON'T KNOW THE ANSWER

Some of the craziest responses I've seen in meetings have come from agency folks who don't have the answer to a question.

It could be a question they'd never thought of. It could be something that's totally outside of their expertise. It could be about a topic they're suddenly, painfully, stomach-churningly aware that they should know about.

Whatever it is, the simple fact is that they don't know the answer.

And, for reasons I will never fully understand, they try to lie.

They make up some absurd shit. Or suddenly pretend they don't speak English. Or fake a heart attack.

STOP GETTING STUMPED

But if you don't know the answer, all you have to say is the following:

"I don't know.. (and this is the critical part) ...but I will find out."

You don't have to be the sum of all earthly knowledge to have the respect of your clients. You simply have to be a resource.

And there's an incredible amount of confidence and active listening that's on display when you acknowledge that your client has asked a great question. You'll get points for wanting to think seriously about it, as opposed to just riffing and moving on.

Like other parts of the toolkit, how exactly you phrase this is up to you. I've said the above phrase word-for-word.

I've said, *"I'm pretty sure I have the answer, but I can already hear the Developers faintly screaming that I'm going to get it wrong, so let me check with them."*

I've said, *"That's a really great question, and it isn't one we considered. Let me check with the rest of the team and get back to you with our thoughts."*

There's a million ways to respond to questions you don't know the answer to.

Lying is never one of them.

Wrong number

I was once part of a new business pitch where the agency CEO tried to pretend we had a "satellite office" in NYC.

(We didn't. What we had was one employee who actually commuted 90 minutes out of the city each morning.)

PROSPECT: You said you're local. Where's your office?

CEO: Oh, [gives the employee's address]

PROSPECT: ...Isn't that an apartment building?

We didn't win the business.

You play how you practice
Watch any interview with any athlete of note, and they'll tell you about how much time they spend practicing.

Taking the same shot over and over and over, until it becomes second nature. Running the same play until they know exactly where their teammates will be without looking. Reacting to conditions almost before they can think, because they've trained until their actions become automatic.

You can do the same, as long as you put in the work.

Your *"Oh Sh*t Toolkit"* can't save you if you don't practice it.

Craft those best-case responses for worst-cast scenarios, then practice them with all the passion of an aspiring MVP. Then you'll have the mental muscle memory to react naturally in the moment. Just like the pros.

STOP GETTING STUMPED

Play the "Um Game" until you have your speechless response down cold.

Go through old decks and delete random slides, then present out loud and treat the missing content as a tech fail.

Watch Jeopardy! And tell Ken Jennings, "I don't know, but I will find out" in response to every answer you don't know the question to.

You want these to become the phrases you think of when your brain stops thinking. And with practice, that's exactly what will happen.

STOP FIGHTING WITH (OR CAVING TO) CLIENTS

In my entire creative career, I've had work approved without any changes exactly twice. And even that is a statistical improbability.

Critique is a part of creative presentation. So it's weird how poorly most folks handle it.

I've seen agencies and creatives fight like hell for an idea that was clearly never going to happen. I've watched as they've begged forgiveness for presenting an idea before the client even had a chance to comment on it.

But before we can start to correct these behaviors, we need to perform a mental mindshift. A cliche-ectomy.

It's time to learn the first rule of Client Fight Club.

START LEARNING THE FIRST RULE OF CLIENT FIGHT CLUB

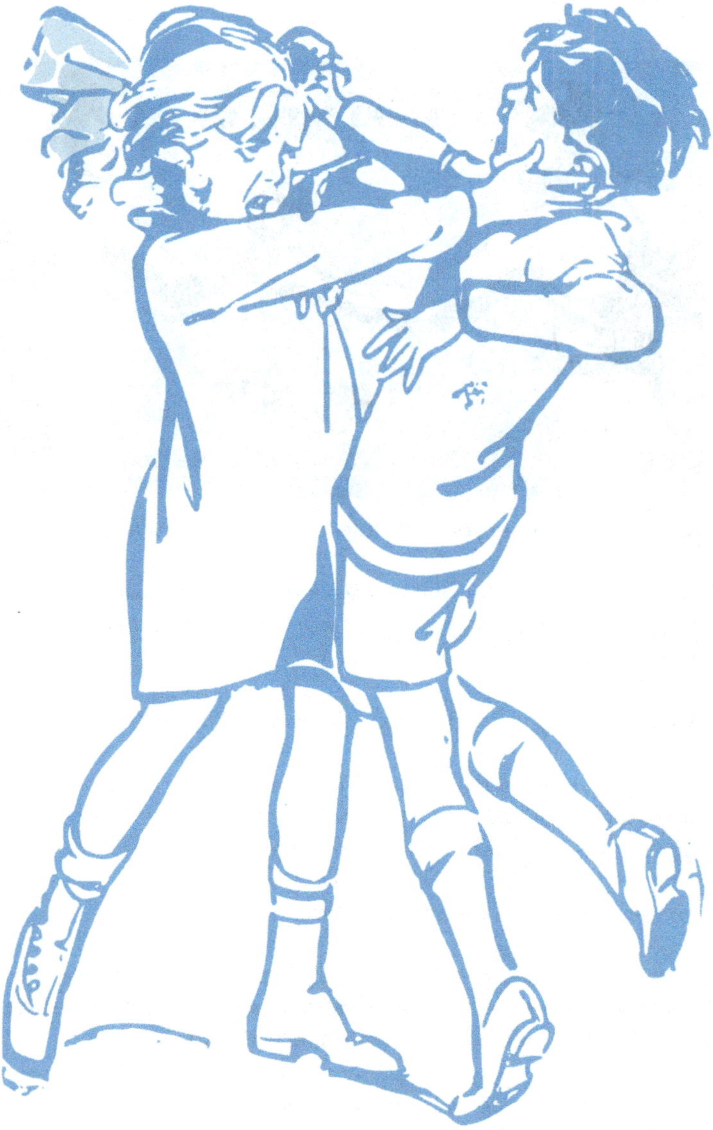

START
LEARNING THE FIRST RULE OF CLIENT FIGHT CLUB

FIRST RULE OF CLIENT FIGHT CLUB:

YOU'RE IN THE WRONG CLUB

As an agency-type, you walk into every meeting thinking:

"I'm a creative genius, and every client is a cliché-loving moron who wouldn't know good work if it bit them in the quarterly earnings."

But you should know that your client is walking in thinking:

"I'm a grown-ass professional, and every creative is a whiny Mac-obsessed hippie who wouldn't last a day at a real job and is just looking to grow their portfolio, or win an award or both."

I'm paraphrasing a bit on both parts.

The point is that both sides of this meeting are predisposed to get annoyed when an objection is raised. The creatives because their vision is misunderstood. The clients because their needs feel ignored.

There's a perfect storm brewing before anyone asks a single question.

STOP FIGHTING WITH (OR CAVING TO) CLIENTS

Whether a client hates the entire strategy or is just questioning a single line, your first move in any fight is to do the last thing they'd ever expect.

Show you're on their side.

Common enemies make friends
In life (especially in those parts of life involving creative discussions) it's a real short hop from "diverging opinions" to "fight or flight" emotions.

If you want to have a productive conversation, you've got to defuse that reaction.

Show them that it's not Agency vs Client.
It's Agency & Client vs The Client's Problem.

Prove to them -and yourself- that you share the same goal. All you're really trying to figure out is the best way to achieve it.

> **Your goal is not to sell your work.**
>
> **Your goal is to solve their problem.**
>
> (your work is just probably the best way to do that)

Do that, and the parts you need to discuss can be…well, a discussion. As opposed to an ego-filled rant about logo sizes.

So the next time things are about to go very wrong, remember the First Rule of Client Fight Club: You're in the wrong club.

START ABOLISHING THE MYTH OF THE DUMB CLIENT

While we're kicking clichés in the teeth, stop me if you've heard this one before…

You didn't win the pitch. Maybe it was a phone call. Maybe it was clear before you even left the conference room. And you're not even back at your desk before someone says:

"They don't get it."

"They're not ready for it."

"It's too good for them anyway."

Everyone, and I mean everyone, says it at one point or another. I used to say it a lot early in my career. Creative work is an emotional, personal endeavor. No matter how much you try to remove yourself from it, it hurts when someone else doesn't feel the way you do about it. So everyone says those words, at one point or another, in the heat of the moment.

But do you believe them?

I love stand up comedy. Like most creative pursuits, it's inherently personal and often judged by its mass appeal. But if a comedian bombs, they don't walk off stage saying, *"That audience was too dumb."*

They have to face the cold, hard truth that their work didn't connect. The jokes didn't land. And they can't show up the next night and do the same things that didn't work the first time. They have to take a long, painful look at their material to learn, grow, and do better next time.

STOP FIGHTING WITH (OR CAVING TO) CLIENTS

What's this got to do with creative presentations? My point is that in almost every case, clients:

"Don't get it" because it wasn't explained in ways they could understand.

"Weren't ready" because no one prepared them for it.

Or the work was *"too good"* because a great idea is terrifying. Unique. Perspective-altering. It is the conceptual equivalent of a tactical nuke. And you just lobbed it into the meeting without proper safety gear or even an instruction manual. How are clients supposed to react?

This is a really important truth to face. Because once you do, you realize…

There are no dumb clients.

I can already hear the screaming. I know, I know- I haven't met your client. But I don't have to.

Because (say it with me now) there are no dumb clients.

There are scared clients (who need you to guarantee them, reassure them, and have their back as you build an idea that's never been done).

There are inexperienced clients (who need you to start at the beginning- nope, even further back than that- and help them understand this thing that is your expertise but totally alien to them).

There are bad clients (who may gaslight you or your company, insult you or your team, or throw you under the bus at every opportunity).

But none of those are dumb clients.

They're all difficult (hell, practically every client is difficult in some way) but it's your job to communicate your creativity in a way that they can understand. To address their needs. Your work should already do that. Otherwise, it's not great work.

But what's obvious to you may not be to them, and it's that disconnect that kills the best ideas. Hence, clients "not getting" your unmitigated genius.

But they're not supposed to. After all, this isn't their area of expertise. It's yours.

To reiterate: It's not them. It's you. And that's fantastic news! Because when you're the problem, you're the solution.

"Hang on, Baldy," I hear you say, *"Just where do you get off saying I'm the problem?"*

Listen, you want to be the problem in this scenario. Here's why:

If you're the difference between success and failure, then success is within your control.

It's difficult- often impossible- to fix your audience. But you can fix your response.

[Insert Middle Finger Here]

In one of the most difficult meetings I've ever had, a client sitting three feet from me insulted the ideas in particular, the agency in general, and me personally. In that order.

Luckily, I knew the first rule of Client Fight Club. So about twenty minutes later, that same client said, *"I'm adding another 50% to your budget."*

That's right. The work died, and we got paid extra to stay on the job. All because I knew the First Rule of Client Fight Club.

Oh, and I had a Plan C. I'll share it with you on the next page.

254

STOP FIGHTING WITH (OR CAVING TO) CLIENTS

START HANDLING OBJECTIONS CONFIDENTLY

This is the three (sometimes three-point-five) step process that has saved ideas, business, and my sanity more than anything else in my career.

This is how I've had every idea die, and still won the pitch.

How I've lost the campaign and still increased the budget.

How I've resurrected ideas that the client killed, then gotten them to pay double for the privilege of making the work. (True story.)

These aren't isolated incidents. My father used to tell me, *"If you can't do something 9 times out of 10, you can't do it."*

I haven't kept an exact count. But at this point it's clear this isn't luck. It's a repeatable result. And more importantly (for you) it's a teachable one.

Welcome to *Plan C*. The one you use when anything (or everything) goes wrong.

Step 1: Ask Questions and Empathize
As creatives and agencies, we're used to treating concept critique as an attack. Some folks will respond with a desperate need to disprove or defend. Others will take the opposite approach and fold like a house of cards, which isn't any better.

The point is that challenges to the work shouldn't be seen as a threat.

They should be seen as a mystery.

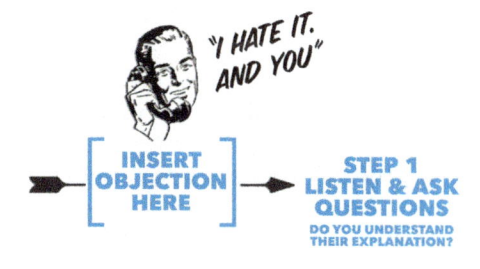

[INSERT OBJECTION HERE] → **STEP 1 LISTEN & ASK QUESTIONS** — *"I HATE IT. AND YOU"* — DO YOU UNDERSTAND THEIR EXPLANATION?

The truth is, most client feedback is pretty mysterious anyway. Take these common objections:

- "I don't like it."
- "We've done it before."
- "That's off brand."
- "We can't afford that."

I've heard all of these in meetings. And watched the agency jump through whatever hoop they thought was appropriate so quickly it looked like an experiment in teleportation.

But what the hell do any of those really mean?

The one certainty is that the client isn't convinced. But don't look at that as a hurdle to be overcome. Instead, view it as the first clue uncovered in a mystery.

For one example, let's take *"We've done it before."*

This one hurts because it looks like you also didn't do your homework on the brand. I've watched folks bow and beg apologies after hearing this. I take a different route:

CLIENT: We've done it before.

ME: Really? How did it perform?

CLIENT: Not great.

ME: How long ago was this? Where did it run?

CLIENT: Well, it wasn't a whole campaign like this. It was actually a black and white newspaper ad. I think it ran on a Tuesday, three years ago? But the headline was sort of saying the same thing.

ME: Ok. And was it using this same insight?

STOP FIGHTING WITH (OR CAVING TO) CLIENTS

CLIENT: Well…kinda? Maybe not? I think that one headline just reminds me of it.

ME: We can lose that headline if you think it'll be a problem. But I feel like there's enough differences here that we can expect a different outcome.

CLIENT: Yeah, I think I just…I have PTSD from that newspaper ad.

Ah. There it is.

"I have PTSD from something else that wasn't this, but I felt like it was, and…this is a totally subjective complaint."

By making the client explain the full and transparent reasoning behind their concerns, you often discover they're not nearly as dramatic or sweeping as they sound. And you're able to prove that to them in the process.

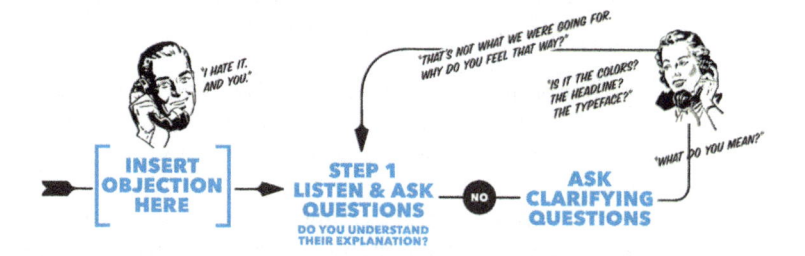

[INSERT OBJECTION HERE] → STEP 1 LISTEN & ASK QUESTIONS (DO YOU UNDERSTAND THEIR EXPLANATION?) — NO — ASK CLARIFYING QUESTIONS

"I HATE IT. AND YOU."
"THAT'S NOT WHAT WE WERE GOING FOR. WHY DO YOU FEEL THAT WAY?"
"IS IT THE COLORS? THE HEADLINE? THE TYPEFACE?"
"WHAT DO YOU MEAN?"

Keep in mind clients aren't doing this on purpose. They haven't spent years analyzing creative work and their own biases. Often, they think they are being clear. You just have to help them express themselves better.

It's 50% Sherlock, 50% Freud, and 100% makes you feel like Batman.

So ask them to explain. It shows you're listening. That you care. And that you're willing to entertain the idea the client may have useful input into the discussion.

I tend to open with a version of the following:

"Ok, that obviously wasn't the reaction we were hoping for. What feels off about it?"

Or

"Ok, what is it that's giving you that feeling?"

Keep in mind your clients are not creatives. They could have a really hard time articulating what it is that they don't like. You may need to give them suggestions based on their initial reaction. So if they said, *"It doesn't feel like the brand,"* you can ask *"Is it the additional colors? The layout? The logo placement?"*

The important thing here is to validate their right to an opinion (even if it's wrong), and to get as much information as you can about it. This step alone will often lower the tension considerably.

Plus, I've lost count of the number of times that new insights, requirements, or understanding came from asking the client to expand on what they didn't like. It might not be comfortable, but it will always be valuable.

STOP FIGHTING WITH (OR CAVING TO) CLIENTS

A sword, double-edged

An ECD I know would always coach his team to *"go where the emotion is"* in a meeting.

"If the client's laughing, stay on the joke. If they're thoughtful, encourage that seriousness." he'd say. *"But that means, if they're angry, you have to go there too.*

You have to sit in that. Accept it. It's the only way you'll be able to move past it."

Often, just getting in the habit of responding to feedback with a question is enormously difficult. Which is why I have folks practice it in my workshop sessions.

PRACTICE EXERCISE: NO FIGHTING

What you'll need

- A sparring partner to play client (preferably someone who's been in critique before)
- A simple concept to present
- Something to dull the PTSD for you both afterwards

What you'll do

Present the work. Don't make it long. It's just a structure for the "client" to respond to.

Once you're done, the "client" will fire off some critique. It can be moderate or scathing. Your goal is to do one thing, and one thing only- respond with an initial question.

You may be shocked how hard it is to stop yourself from defending or solving the critique. But that's why this is such a valuable drill.

Like I said when preparing to improvise: you play how you practice.

Step 2: Work backwards to find common ground
Once you understand the nature of their complaint, I want you to start explaining your motivation.

This is not the same as defending the work. This is you explaining the reason the work was done.

Not *"We think blue was a strong compliment to your brand colors,"* but *"This was a Fall promotion, so we wanted to bring in some colors that spoke to the season."*

Your goal here is to align on the motivation, the reason, behind the work. If they don't agree with your reasoning, step further back.

This also serves a second purpose- it reminds the client that you're not as far apart as it may seem.

That's important because, in this moment, there's been a slight breach of trust. They expected one thing, you showed them another. Reminding them that you're still aligned on the issues before this reminds them that you're not as far off from success as they may feel in that moment.

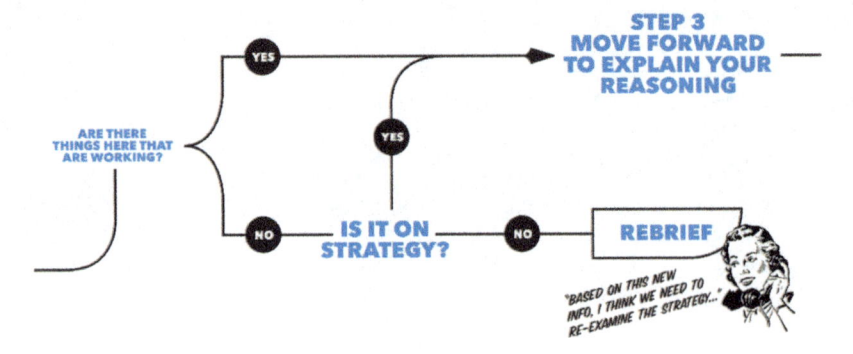

260

In extreme cases, you may wind up all the way back at the brief. (This is where the "point five" step comes in.)

You'll know you're here when no alignment has been found, and you have to ask a question like, *"Is the main purpose of this messaging still to promote the Fall offer, or is there something more important?"*

In these cases, the work is dead. The goal posts have been moved (or perhaps were never built in the first place) and trying to sell them on the work you brought is a fool's errand. Lose the battle to win the war.

Remember the meeting I opened this section with, where the client stopped me on slide two and told me they hated everything only to hand us a fifty-percent budget increase twenty minutes later? Yeah, that work was dead. There was no way it wasn't.

But because I worked backwards to try and find common ground, it became obvious that the client had mis-briefed us. Asking questions helped them realize that, and got us aligned on the goals they actually wanted to achieve. So they decided to pay us more to solve both the strategic issue and deliver the creative.

Note that you don't want to go further back than necessary. This isn't about beating them over the head with all the things you agree on. Once you find common ground, you're ready for the final step.

Step 3: Work forwards to explain your process

You've listened and asked questions. You've made sure you're aligned on the rationale. Now you can defend your choices.

Jumping to this step directly is what instigates a "you vs them" argument. But if you've gone through the previous steps, this is now merely a conversation about the best ways to achieve a specific aspect of the work.

And it's okay to have this conversation because you've shown them through steps one and two that it's not your opinion vs theirs. It's you and them vs the problem you're both eager to solve. You're simply explaining how you came to your conclusion and asking if they feel any differently about it now that you've discussed the reasons behind it.

"I understand the work felt off for X reason. We all agree something has to be done to address Y motivation, which was why we made this choice with the work. Does that still feel off for X reason?"

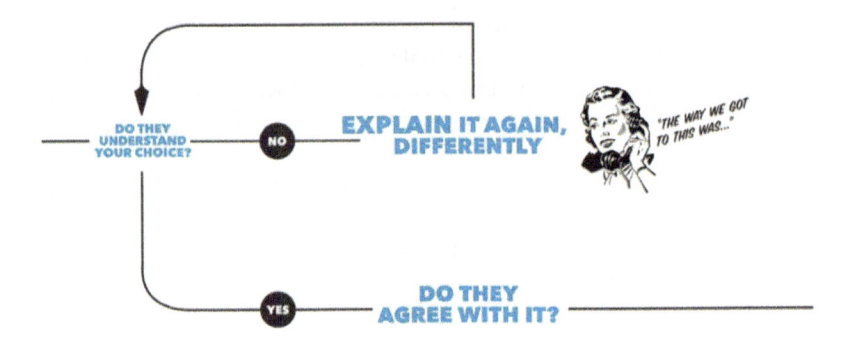

DO THEY UNDERSTAND YOUR CHOICE? — **NO** — **EXPLAIN IT AGAIN, DIFFERENTLY** *"THE WAY WE GOT TO THIS WAS..."*

YES — **DO THEY AGREE WITH IT?**

Again, you want to make sure that your reasoning is clear. Not that they necessarily agree with it. You're asking if an honest re-evaluation (now that motivations and context are better understood) changes anything.

262

You just want to make sure they understand there was a method to your madness. You're not some foppish artiste who makes design choices whacked out on absinthe.

But do they agree with you? From here, you get one of three answers:

"NOT ENTIRELY!"

They totally get where you're coming from now. You totally get where they're coming from now. As a result, the change they're asking for is actually much smaller than originally stated.

Going from "This sucks, we hate it" to "Ok, so just change the last sentence in the second paragraph" is a massive, massive victory.

While the significance of the compromise will vary, this is actually the most common outcome I have using this framework.

If it's the one you end up with, be proud.

"NOT AT ALL!"

You can't win 'em all. In this scenario, they get where you're coming from and respect you more for the process you just went through together. But they still want their changes made.

This might seem like the "worst" outcome, but again, sometimes you have to lose the battle to win the war.

I've had campaigns die because they were unsalvageable. But using this framework allowed me to deepen the relationship with the client, and we were actually awarded more work in the end.

I've also been in meetings where we "ran away" after the client was mad about the work, promising additional concepts as we fled. But without any additional information, we had no idea how to course correct. With this approach, even if you're busted back to the brief, you'll have the information you need to nail it this time.

STOP FIGHTING WITH (OR CAVING TO) CLIENTS

If this is where you wind up, here's a tip on how to end your meeting. Recap where you went wrong (so they know you know), restate the plan you have to move forward, and clarify exactly what they'll see next round.

That way, you can be 100% certain there are no surprises when you come back together, and they'll sleep a little easier in the interim.

Of course, there is a third scenario…

They totally get where you're coming from now, and retract their complaint. As you were.

This is awesome. You're awesome. High fives all around.

However, please try to resist screaming, *"Ah ha! I was right all along!"*

"I HATE IT. AND YOU."

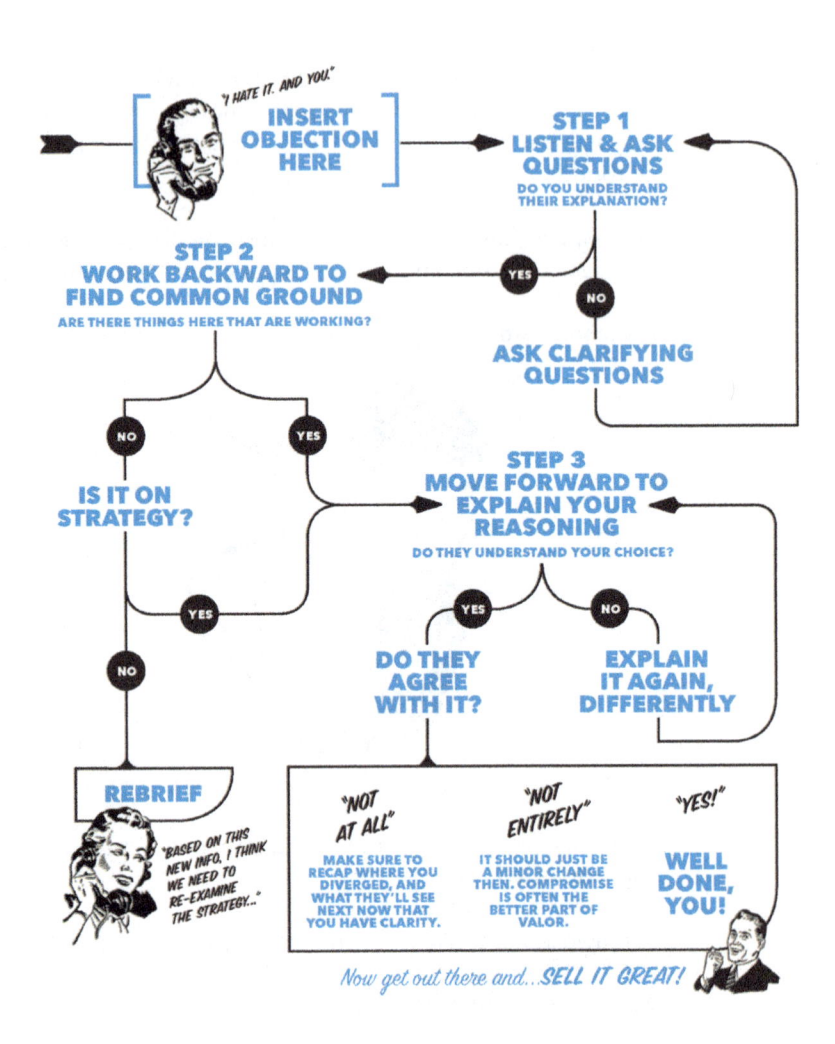

[INSERT OBJECTION HERE]

STEP 1
LISTEN & ASK QUESTIONS
DO YOU UNDERSTAND THEIR EXPLANATION?

- YES →
- NO → **ASK CLARIFYING QUESTIONS**

STEP 2
WORK BACKWARD TO FIND COMMON GROUND
ARE THERE THINGS HERE THAT ARE WORKING?

- NO → **IS IT ON STRATEGY?**
  - YES →
  - NO → **REBRIEF** — "BASED ON THIS NEW INFO, I THINK WE NEED TO RE-EXAMINE THE STRATEGY..."
- YES →

STEP 3
MOVE FORWARD TO EXPLAIN YOUR REASONING
DO THEY UNDERSTAND YOUR CHOICE?

- YES → **DO THEY AGREE WITH IT?**
- NO → **EXPLAIN IT AGAIN, DIFFERENTLY**

"NOT AT ALL" — MAKE SURE TO RECAP WHERE YOU DIVERGED, AND WHAT THEY'LL SEE NEXT NOW THAT YOU HAVE CLARITY.

"NOT ENTIRELY" — IT SHOULD JUST BE A MINOR CHANGE THEN. COMPROMISE IS OFTEN THE BETTER PART OF VALOR.

"YES!" — WELL DONE, YOU!

Now get out there and... SELL IT GREAT!

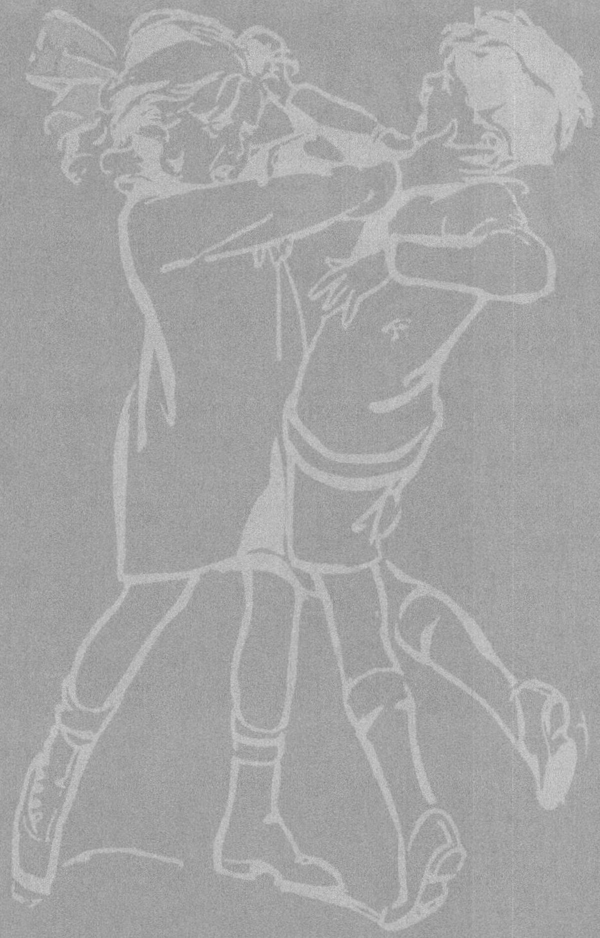

STOP TAKING OBJECTIONS AT FACE VALUE

Remember that story about my ECD who asked, *"And what will you do if they say 'No'?"* The truth is, all of us know what client objections sound like.

If you combine the skills we've talked about in *Start Preparing to Improvise* with the techniques just covered in *Start Handling Objections*, you can create a tool for just about anything a client says.

That might seem impossible. After all, a client could say practically anything at any time. But if you stop and think about the questions behind the words, that list becomes significantly smaller.

START RECOGNIZING FIFTY PHRASES THAT KILL CREATIVITY

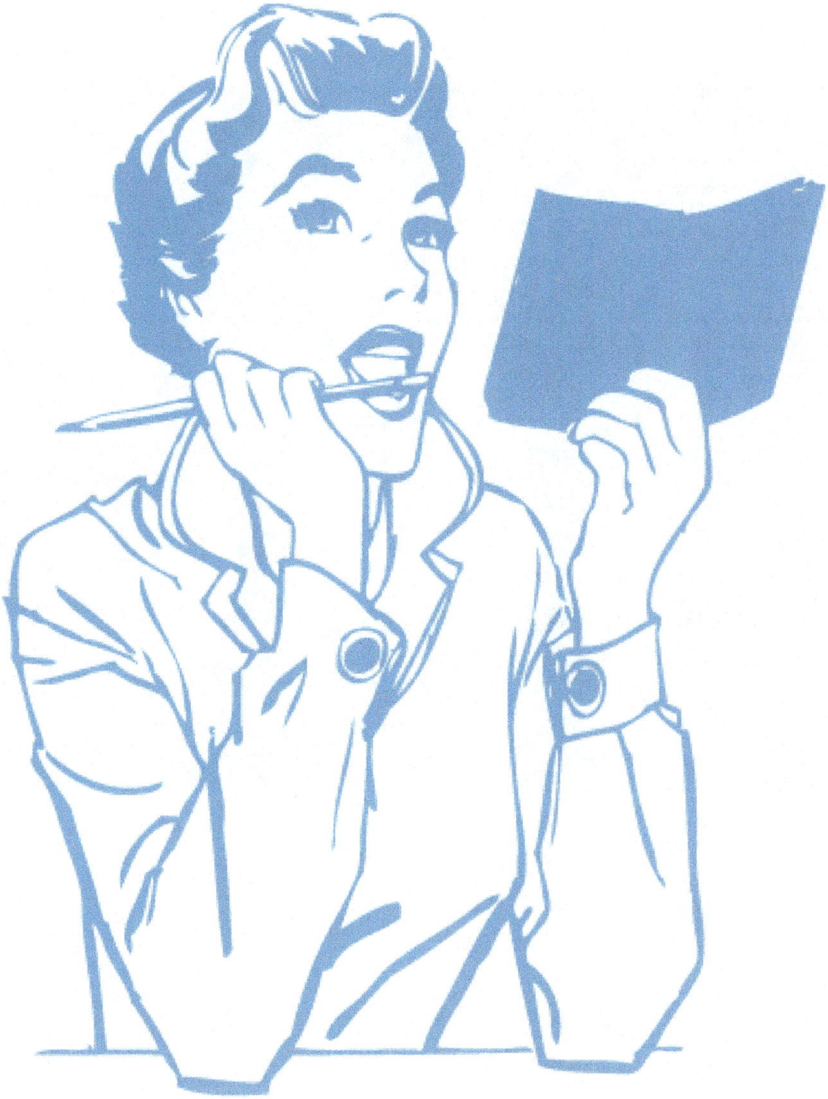

Custom Cheesesteaks

During one memorable occasion, a client of mine was making a case for why we should move away from the clichéd imagery of Cheesesteaks to advertise the city of Philadelphia.

One of her coworkers (playing client) called out, *"Oh, I love those cheesesteak ads! They're the best!"*

(This is perhaps the most savage coworker-on-coworker violence I've ever seen as a coach)

The rest of the room started laughing, and the presenter was struck speechless.

When the various death threats were done being thrown around, I pointed out how the presenter could have responded: *"Those cheesesteak ads have worked well for us to date. But we know that we've got the cheesesteak fans on lock. If we want to expand, we need to do something for all the people that hasn't worked for."*

"Sure, Ben, that would have been great. But I'm not that fast."

But you and I know I'm not that fast either.

And of course I haven't practiced my "Cheesesteak-Loving Client" response in the mirror 100 times.

What I have prepared is a way to acknowledge my client's love for an existing campaign, while explaining why we still needed something different.

You know, that thing that happens all the time in our meetings?

I just filled in the blank with "cheesesteak" and I was set.

272

TAKING OBJECTIONS AT FACE VALUE

The trick is to identify the common pain points and issues behind these statements, and address those.

It wasn't about cheesesteaks. It was about acknowledging personal bias and past efforts, while making room for new work.

Things like this are always said in agency hallways and client meetings. Here's a list of fifty of them (originally collected by Dave DuFours), along with what I believe they really mean, and how you can address them.

I bet you've heard them all before:

START
RECOGNIZING FIFTY PHRASES THAT KILL CREATIVITY

1. Our place is different.
2. We tried that before.
3. It costs too much.
4. That's not my job.
5. They're too busy to do that.
6. We don't have the time.
7. Not enough help.
8. It's too radical a change.
9. The staff will never buy it.
10. It's against company policy.
11. The union will scream.
12. That will run up our overhead.
13. We don't have the authority.
14. Let's get back to reality.
15. That's not our problem.
16. I don't like the idea.
17. I'm not saying you're wrong but...
18. You're two years ahead of your time.
19. Now's not the right time.
20. It isn't in the budget.
21. Can't teach an old dog new tricks.
22. Good thought, but impractical.
23. Let's give it more thought.
24. We'll be the laughingstock of the industry.
25. Not that again.
26. Where'd you dig that one up?
27. We did alright without it before.
28. It's never been tried.
29. Let's put that one on the back burner for now.
30. Let's form a committee.
31. It won't work in our place.
32. The executive committee will never go for it.
33. I don't see the connection.
34. Let's all sleep on it.
35. It can't be done.
36. It's too much trouble to change.

TAKING OBJECTIONS AT FACE VALUE

37. It won't pay for itself.
38. It's impossible.
39. I know a person who tried it and got fired.
40. We've always done it this way.
41. We'd lose money in the long run.
42. Don't rock the boat.
43. That's what we can expect from the staff.
44. Has anyone else ever tried it?
45. Let's look into it further.
46. We'll have to answer to the stockholders.
47. Quit dreaming.
48. If it ain't broke, don't fix it.
49. That's too much ivory tower.
50. It's too much work.

Ok. Take a second, shake off the trauma, and get ready to learn how to flip every one of these phrases like a linguistic judo master.

The first thing to realize is that these aren't fifty separate phrases. In fact, most of them are different ways of saying the same eight objections. Check it out.

CATEGORY 1: CHANGE IS SCARY

This is perhaps the largest category of objections on the list. Some of them pass off the blame (*"The staff will never buy it"*), others are firmly based on self-preservation (*"Someone got fired for that"*), and some are pretty honest (*"It's too radical a change"*).

1. Our place is different.
9. The staff will never buy it.
8. It's too radical a change.
11. The union will scream.
13. We don't have the authority.
14. Let's get back to reality.
21. Can't teach an old dog new tricks.

24. We'll be the laughingstock of the industry.
25. Not that again.
31. It won't work in our place.
32. The executive committee will never go for it.
39. I know a person who tried it and got fired.
40. We've always done it this way.
42. Don't rock the boat.
46. We'll have to answer to the stockholders.
24. We'll be the laughingstock of the industry.

My Response:
"Is [the goal] still the goal?" or "Do we still want [the goal]?"

Presumably, your brief outlines what the client is trying to accomplish with this work. This is the time to ask if it's truly the most important thing. If it is, then reminding them of this fact will reinforce that we're not arguing about the goal, merely the method. And you won't get somewhere different by doing the same thing.

Often, this brings some honest clarity to an assignment that didn't have it to begin with.

CLIENT: *"Well, we do want [the goal] but we need the buy-in of so-and-so, and they'll never go for it."*

YOU: *"Ok, but if this is the goal, what do we need to do in order to convince them?"*

As you continue down this track, one of two things will happen. You'll either get them to stand up for what they asked for, or they'll move the goalposts. If it's the first, great. If it's the second, at least you can get back to work with an accurate endpoint in mind.

CATEGORY 2: CASH RULES EVERYTHING

Ah, the almighty dollar. We'd love to do the work, you see. It's just not in the budget. Frankly, I could quadruple the size of this category without even trying. But these four are demoralizing enough.

These can be thrown at you in two ways. The first is apologetically. The second is a cold, hard "No." In either case, the answer is the same.

3. It costs too much.
12. That will run up our overhead.
20. It isn't in the budget.
37. It won't pay for itself.

My Response:
"Ok. But if you could afford it, would you do it?"

This forces the client to admit/clarify whether price is the real problem, or if they're just incapable of telling you they don't like it.

If they do like it, then you're just negotiating what both sides can do to make it happen. Maybe there are ways to save on costs. Maybe the client will set up a meeting with whoever holds the checkbook on their end. But rather than get lost in purgatory, we've agreed the idea is a go. We're just working out details.

In other words, this just became You and Client vs Client's Problem and Budgetary Constraints.

CATEGORY 3: CAN'T BE BOTHERED

This is often an internal objection, but you can hear it from your clients too. Particularly if your concept involves them innovating or adjusting their offer.

4. That's not my job.
5. They're too busy to do that.
6. We don't have the time.
7. Not enough help.
22. Good thought, but impractical.
36. It's too much trouble to change.
50. It's too much work.

My Response:
"If we can find a way to make it work without extra effort, would you do it?"

Like the response to the previous category, this is about clarifying whether or not effort is the real objection. Often, you'll be met with a list of all the reasons it's not doable. So you might have to repeat this one a few ways. *"Ok, but let's live in Fantasy Land for a moment- assuming this wouldn't impact your process, would you do it?"* Because, again, at that point the idea is bought. We're just figuring out logistics.

And if it's really a "No"? Then at least we've saved time and effort.

CATEGORY 4: DELAYING TACTICS

Sometimes, these lines are meant in good faith. *"There's something there, but I'm not sure it's refined yet. Let's give it more thought."* is completely different from *"Thanks for the work. Let's give it more thought."*

23. Let's give it more thought.
29. Let's put that one on the back burner for now.
30. Let's form a committee.
34. Let's all sleep on it.
45. Let's look into it further.

My Response:
"What do we still need to figure out?"

Like the original objection, this response can either be a straightforward request or a challenge. In either case, it's forcing the client to sharpen their meandering, vague feedback into something you can work with.

If they can't articulate it, try and help them. Remember that you've had training and experience communicating these things. They probably went to business school.

CATEGORY 5: UNWORTHY OBJECTIONS

These are a crafty set of responses. That's because they often praise the thinking behind the work while simultaneously dismissing it. The backhanded compliment can throw you off your game if you're unprepared.

18. You're two years ahead of your time.
19. Now's not the right time.
31. It won't work in our place.

My Response:
"Why do you say that?" or "What would need to change to make it right?"

When facing this, I want to be very clear where the client thinks the disconnect is. Maybe there's something in their offering that will change soon, but it's not revealed yet (rare). In that case, I'll push to bring this back when the time is right.

But usually, it's that they're scared of the work. This can often arise when a mid-tier category player is shown top-tier work for the first time. They recognize it as the sort of thing their competition is running but are also facing (for the first time) just how big the gap is between who they are and who they want to be.

So, after you help them understand that, be sure to bring some examples. Case studies of similar evolutions. Times that other companies have benefited from making similarly large swings.

Help them understand that what they're feeling isn't unique. If they want to get where they want to go, it starts right now.

CATEGORY 6: HISTORY REPEATING

I've actually gotten a plethora of phrases that all come down to, "It's been done." Below are just two of them.

2. We tried that before.
43. That's what we can expect from the staff.

My Response:
"Do you have an example?" or "Can you tell me about it?"

There's a ton of nuance to this response, and you want to wade into the details. Sometimes what they mean is that a similar headline was produced once six years ago. Just explain it's not the same as your entire campaign.

Sometimes, it's that they've tried something they think is like what you've presented, but you understand the differences. Share with them how this time will be different (broader reach, more budget, etc).

And sometimes, they're right. That's actually been done before. In which case, admit you didn't know and ask them for as much detail about the good and the bad as possible. It'll be useful information to have when you come back to the table.

CATEGORY 7: UNNECESSARY RESPONSES

These amount to *"Can we do less?"* and are basically a subconscious acknowledgement of fear.

27. We did alright without it before.
28. It's never been tried.
24. We'll be the laughingstock of the industry.

My Response:
"What are your goals?"

These are funny to me, because they're based on a false premise. After all, something is wrong. If it was all perfect, you wouldn't be having this meeting.

So there's got to be a difference you're trying to achieve. And to paraphrase a really smart guy- You're not gonna get new results doing the same shit.

So I make 'em say the truth out loud. And then point out that no one minds being the laughingstock of the industry when they increase profits.

CATEGORY 7: UNNECESSARY RESPONSES

Look, I love hyperbole just as much as the next person. But you should know that if you come at me with an absolute, there better be some peer-reviewed science to back it up.

26. Where'd you dig that one up?
35. It can't be done.
38. It's impossible.
47. Quit dreaming.

My Response:
"What makes you say that?"

I ask this because it's possible (however unlikely) that there is some legitimate reason it can't be done. I've worked in a lot of tech and healthcare, and there are limits and regulations to each. Sometimes they get in the way of our ideas.

But usually? Usually what they're really saying is, *"We haven't done that before."* Or some other objection on this list. And you know what to do with those.

THE SINGLES

A collection of specific responses to specific phrases.

33. I don't see the connection.

My Response:
[Restate the insight]

This is pretty honest feedback. What's important is to understand it isn't *"No,"* it's *"I don't get it."* So help them get it.

If someone's using this as a snarky remark to try and shut you down, ask them if they want you to explain it a different way. They'll usually switch tactics immediately, which is a sign their objection has nothing to do with your connection or lack thereof.

10. It's against company policy.

My Response:
"Ignoring that for the moment- would you still do the idea if you could?"

If they just hate the idea, let's not get into company policy. But if they do like it and simply can't see how it's going to work within the current system, start brainstorming with them.

Sometimes this really does kill the idea. But sometimes it just makes you and your direct client against the world. Which can be a pretty cool place to be.

15. That's not our problem.

My Response:
"What is the problem?" or "Isn't the problem [insert here]?"

You need to listen to them at this point. Because odds are this feedback came during the strategy. And if that's off, there's no reason to even share the creative.

Sometimes it comes during a creative idea. In which case, you need to help them see why it solves the problem you both agree they have.

16. I don't like the idea.

My Response:
"What don't you like about it?"

Truthfully, this is a whole category in itself. There's a hundred ways to say this. But your response is the same. You want to hear exactly what they don't like. Because it could just be the size of the logo, and the rest of it is fine. After you've heard their grievances, follow up with *"Is anything working for you?"*

284

TAKING OBJECTIONS AT FACE VALUE

Because sometimes we accidentally throw out the good with the bad.

17. I'm not saying you're wrong but...

My Response:
"..."

I'm not quite sure where this line is going. If the client trailed off, I'd wait them out. If they really had nothing to say, I'd probe for details, like above.

If this is just some asinine prefix added onto some other objection in this list, ignore it and focus on the other objection. Starting with "Well, I appreciate you not *saying* I was wrong…" is– while satisfying– unlikely to help your case.

44. Has anyone else ever tried it?

My Response:
"There's been some similar ideas that we found, but they're different because…" or *"You would be the first. But we have done similarly surprising/impactful/shocking/different executions for other clients."*

The goal here is to reassure them. Either that the campaign they're bankrolling is truly ownable, or that this never-before-attempted insanity isn't as risky as it sounds. Case studies can be great for the latter.

48. If it ain't broke, don't fix it.

My Response:
"What you've done has been perfect for your current audience. But if you want to reach others, you need a different approach."

There's a lot of ways this phrase can live in a meeting. *"But we love our [old campaign name]"* is another. The goal in your response is to acknowledge that the thing they love is great, while pointing out that you can't achieve new results with old actions.

49. That's too much ivory tower.

My Response:
"Wut?"

Honestly, I've never heard this, or heard of it. My interpretation is it's telling me that the idea is too theoretical, and won't actually work in the real world. But I'm not sure. So my actual response would be, *"What do you mean by that?"*

TAKING OBJECTIONS AT FACE VALUE

START TAKING "YES" FOR AN ANSWER

Remember what we said way back in the beginning- the goal of every meeting is just to get to the next one.

If you find yourself in a situation where the client is stuck on something that you're just going to have to rehash later, disengage as politely as possible.

> "That's a key point. Let's get this piece sorted first, and once it's squared away we'll have all the information we need to decide on that."

Imagine you were a realtor selling a house. If a couple walks in and immediately starts arguing about the wall color or where the couch would fit- congratulations. You've sold the house.

They can see themselves in it so clearly that they're arguing currently meaningless details.

The same is true for your work. If you're presenting the concept, and the client is hammering you about potential headlines, don't worry- you've sold the campaign. Your job is to shake their hand and get the hell out of there.

You're just going to have to re-fight all those decisions during production anyhow.

Remember the first rule of Client Fight Club.

START RECOGNIZING THE LIMITS OF MEETINGS

When I coach clients, the conversation starts with general challenges. Then we get into best practices. Then we start talking about the nitty gritty. The exceptions. And then, inevitably, we reach it.

The limits of meetings.

Meetings cannot solve everything. And what I've found is much of the time we're trying to make them solve things they weren't designed for.

"My client hates advertising."

"My client doesn't actually have the budget."

"My client won't stop berating us in the meeting."

"My client keeps asking us to present the same idea but says they're not ready to approve it yet."

These scenarios aren't solved by meetings. They're solved by phone calls.

Here's an example that came up while I was working with one agency.

TAKING OBJECTIONS AT FACE VALUE

Make the call

CD: I don't get it. We love the work. Their dev team is excited about the work. It's just this one guy on their side who won't approve it. He's holding up everything. How do we present this in a way to win him over?

ME: You don't.

CD: What?

ME: Something is off for this guy. Maybe his boss is telling him not to let dev bury themselves in more work. Maybe he's under pressure to get the price down but won't say it out loud. Maybe he's scared of the timeline. There's something he doesn't understand, or you don't understand, that he won't admit to in a meeting. Call him on the phone.

CD: Shouldn't Account do that?

ME: Probably. Do you want to sell the work?

The next week, this CD came to our session ecstatic. He couldn't stop telling me how everything went exactly as I said. He called the guy, discovered some unspoken fears, was able to address them, and everything was approved without another presentation.

There are limits to meetings. Sometimes the solution happens outside of them.

STOP EXPECTING TOO MUCH FROM YOURSELF

If you've read this book, it's a safe bet you care about how your meetings go.

When I work with folks, there's a lot of self-criticism. They understand the systems and frameworks I'm sharing, but struggle to implement them perfectly the first time. And they get frustrated with themselves.

First, that's totally normal. You're not only learning new ways to do something, you're learning dozens of new ways to do dozens of things. So my first recommendation is- do not try to do all this at once.

Change one thing at a time. Make a plan. For example, start with filler words. But not just filler words- I want you to start with simply recognizing when you say them. Then, once you accomplish that, start trying to eliminate them. And if you only catch one or two the first time, that's great. Celebrate that.

Trying to go from where you are to the perfect ideal is like a NASA graduate getting frustrated they can't reach the Moon by jumping. It's a completely ridiculous standard.

START BEING LIKE BRUCE LEE (NOT WATER)

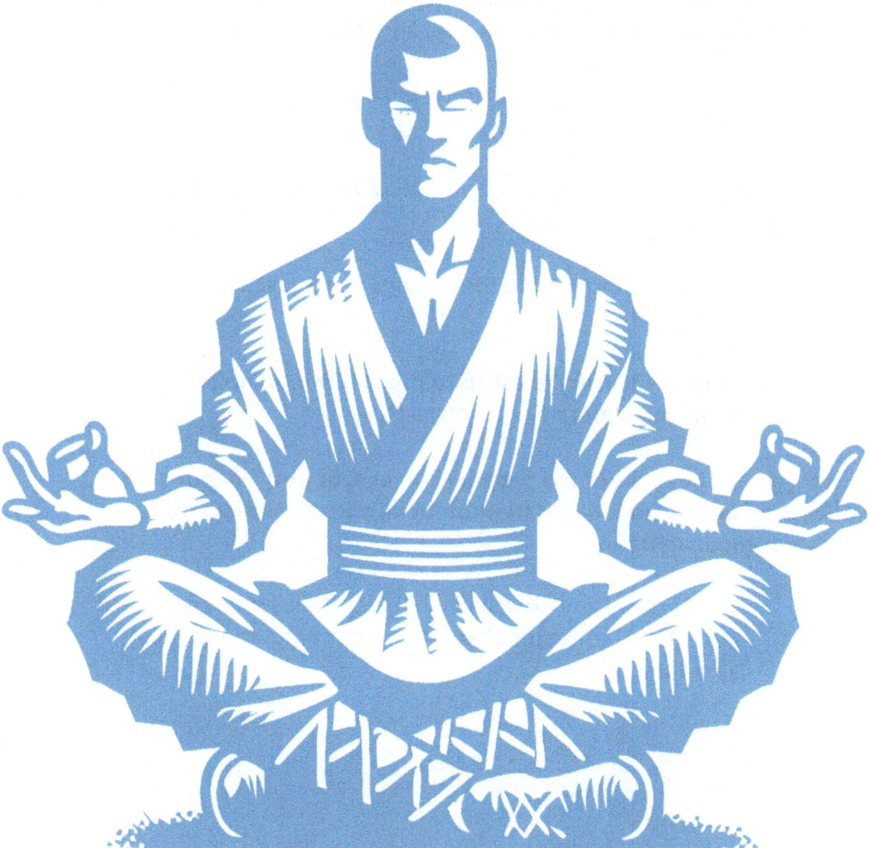

My favorite "Little Dragon" quote has nothing to do with H_2O. It's a much lesser known one, and it goes something like this:

"Before I learned the [martial] art, a punch was just a punch, and a kick, just a kick.

After I learned the art, there were a hundred ways to punch, a hundred ways to kick.

Now that I understand the art, a punch is just a punch and a kick is just a kick."

Initially, when we're asked to present, we go up to the front of a room and start talking. Pretty simple.

Once we get into nuances of the proper slide use, of body language, and of improvisation, standing in front of the room seems almost hopelessly complicated.

But so does any new skill while you're learning it. And at the same time, some jerk like me is coaching you to "Just be yourself."

STOP EXPECTING TOO MUCH FROM YOURSELF

Eventually, you're able to just walk up to the front of a room and start talking again. Except now you're reflexively doing all the things you had to think about before.

You'll get there (I did). Just recognize it's all part of the process.

No matter how good you get at this, there will always be something you wish you could have done differently.

But keep in mind that the bar for a good presentation is so low it might as well just be painted on the sidewalk.

Remember that meetings are pass/fail tests. It's fine to want a good score, but you're just trying to get out of this successfully.

If you want to be critical of your mistakes, that's fine. You just have to be equally and objectively honest with yourself about all the things you did right.

Last Right's

I was doing some freelance work and the agency, knowing a deal when they saw one, also asked me to present the ideas. So I did. It ended with every single member of the client team loving our best idea- except for the president, who was honestly a bit of a dick during the whole thing.

We got off the call, and before anyone could say anything, I blurted out, *"Well, that could have gone better."*

The agency owner was incredulous. *"What are you talking about? That was one of the best meetings I've ever seen!"*

I realized that I was hung up on one particular moment where I handled a comment from the president decently. Decently, but I was already thinking of ways I could have answered better. But the owner was right. The meeting had gone great. I wasn't being fair to myself.

START RECOGNIZING YOU CAN'T WIN 'EM ALL

No matter what you do, sometimes the idea is gonna die. The pitch will be lost. Nothing you tried worked.

None of us win all the time. And good news- sometimes, if you do all of the above and still can't make it work- it means you shouldn't have worked with that client in the first place.

But for me, knowing that I can, and did, use everything at my disposal to sell the best ideas to my clients is what lets me sleep at night.

Veto Power

That last meeting I mentioned? They didn't go with the idea everyone loved.

Turns out that night the President emailed the entire team and essentially said,

"I'm the boss, and we're doing the idea that only I liked."

I heard later on that it was such an insane, egomaniacal move that two people resigned from the company over it.

I felt strangely better after hearing that.

You can't win 'em all. I'll settle for winning all the ones I can.

STOP EXPECTING TOO MUCH FROM YOURSELF

START RECOGNIZING THE BEST PART

When I got really good at presenting, an incredible thing happened. I started walking into rooms and asking my teams, *"We can do this, right? Because I can sell it. I will get the client to buy it. So make sure we can pull this off before I show it to them."*

It's the polar opposite of, "They won't buy that."

Being able to present with confidence is a blank check to the concepting process.

A promise that the only boundary is what's right for the client, not what's sellable. It changes the entire game, and it's the greatest gift you can give to your concepts and your teams.

Now, go sell the shit out of your best ideas.

WITHOUT TALKING LIKE THIS TO YOUR CLIENTS FOR THE NEXT SIX MONTHS.

How's that for a callback?

STOP

Stop thinking this was all me

I have a lot of people I need to thank.

My wife, Jodi, who was the person that told me to quit my job and try this coaching thing.

My children, Molly and Sam, who never miss an opportunity to complain about how bad the speakers are at school. Or about how I talk with my hands.

Dan Nelken and Cameron Day, both of whom I pestered incessantly throughout the process of writing this book. Because they have written their own books, which you should buy if you haven't already.

The various dogs who have forced me to get up from my computer and leave the house for at least a few minutes when working from home. Now stop trying to eat my green screen.

Nikhil Rajagopalan, for editing the initial version of this book. Any appropriate use of grammar, numbers, and semicolons is due to him. He also removed about 4 million uses of the word "so."

Dan Van Wert, for editing the second version of this book with the eyes of an eagle, the patience of a saint, and the meticulousness of a bomb-disposal expert.

Kelly Bartell, for designing the cover. And for giving my business an actual brand.

Julia Ko, for being the adult in the room.

Andy Lawrence, for making these words look prettier than they deserve. Speaking of, this book was laid out using a modular grid, in Avenir Next.

And to everyone else, who believed in me when I didn't believe in myself. Who trusted me with their career, or their people, or both. Thank you. It means more to me than I can say. And that's saying something.

ABOUT THE AUTHOR

As an advertising creative, Ben Levy pulled all-nighters at agencies like StrawberryFrog, HAVAS, and RTO&P. His work for brands like Coca-Cola, Boost Mobile, New Balance, Jägermeister, Virgin America, and others occasionally earned him shiny things.

As a coach, Ben's taught the fine art of persuasion to everyone from creative freelancers to agency execs. He's coached and spoken to folks at shops like Mischief, Droga5, GREY, Ogilvy, Digitas Health, FCB, VML, etc.

He's trained in three forms of martial arts, can slow his heart rate on command, and has an encyclopedic knowledge of Looney Tunes.

Don't be too impressed though, he also managed to fail a Salsa class.

If you'd like to get in touch about coaching or workshops, or want to check out some podcast appearances, you can stalk him at www.sellitgreat.com or search Sell It Great on linkedin.

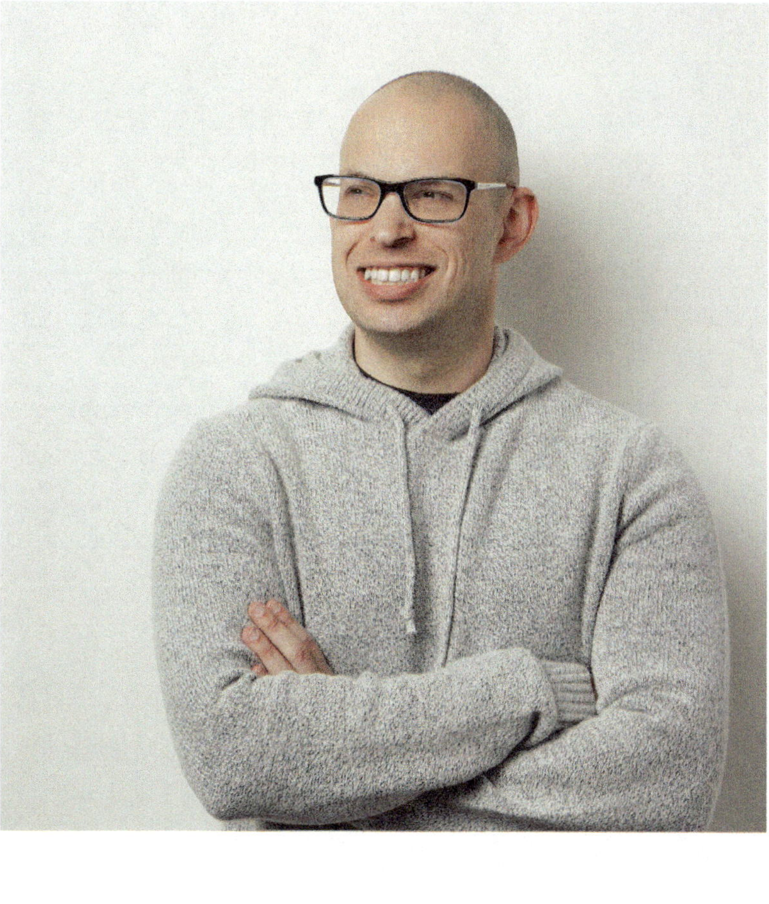

Made in the USA
Las Vegas, NV
19 February 2025